COMMON SENSE

GET IT, USE IT, AND TEACH IT IN THE WORKPLACE

Ken Tanner

Common Sense: Get It, Use It, and Teach It in the Workplace

ISBN-13 (pbk): 978-1-4302-4152-2

ISBN-13 (electronic): 978-1-4302-4153-9

President and Publisher: Paul Manning
Acquisitions Editor: Jeff Olson
Editorial Board: Steve Anglin, Mark Beckner, Ewan Buckingham, Gary Cornell,
    Louise Corrigan, Morgan Ertel, Jonathan Gennick, Jonathan Hassell,
    Robert Hutchinson, Michelle Lowman, James Markham, Matthew Moodie,
    Jeff Olson, Jeffrey Pepper, Douglas Pundick, Ben Renow-Clarke, Dominic Shakeshaft,
    Gwenan Spearing, Matt Wade, Tom Welsh
Coordinating Editor: Rita Fernando
Copy Editor: Cat Ohala
Compositor: SPi Global
Indexer: SPi Global
Cover Designer: Anna Ishchenko

Distributed to the book trade worldwide by Springer Science+Business Media New York, 233 Spring Street, 6th Floor, New York, NY 10013. Phone 1-800-SPRINGER, fax (201) 348-4505, e-mail orders-ny@springer-sbm.com, or visit www.springeronline.com. Apress Media, LLC is a California LLC and the sole member (owner) is Springer Science + Business Media Finance Inc (SSBM Finance Inc). SSBM Finance Inc is a Delaware corporation.

For information on translations, please e-mail rights@apress.com, or visit www.apress.com.

Apress and friends of ED books may be purchased in bulk for academic, corporate, or promotional use. eBook versions and licenses are also available for most titles. For more information, reference our Special Bulk Sales–eBook Licensing web page at www.apress.com/bulk-sales.

Any source code or other supplementary materials referenced by the author in this text is available to readers at www.apress.com. For detailed information about how to locate your book's source code, go to www.apress.com/source-code/.

Apress Business: The Unbiased Source of Business Information

Apress business books provide essential information and practical advice, each written for practitioners by recognized experts. Busy managers and professionals in all areas of the business world—and at all levels of technical sophistication—look to our books for the actionable ideas and tools they need to solve problems, update and enhance their professional skills, make their work lives easier, and capitalize on opportunity.

Whatever the topic on the business spectrum—entrepreneurship, finance, sales, marketing, management, regulation, information technology, among others—Apress has been praised for providing the objective information and unbiased advice you need to excel in your daily work life. Our authors have no axes to grind; they understand they have one job only—to deliver up-to-date, accurate information simply, concisely, and with deep insight that addresses the real needs of our readers.

It is increasingly hard to find information—whether in the news media, on the Internet, and now all too often in books—that is even-handed and has your best interests at heart. We therefore hope that you enjoy this book, which has been carefully crafted to meet our standards of quality and unbiased coverage.

We are always interested in your feedback or ideas for new titles. Perhaps you'd even like to write a book yourself. Whatever the case, reach out to us at editorial@apress.com and an editor will respond swiftly. Incidentally, at the back of this book, you will find a list of useful related titles. Please visit us at www.apress.com to sign up for newsletters and discounts on future purchases.

The Apress Business Team

This book is dedicated to

Dawn Hochsprung

Mary Sherlach

Victoria Soto

Anne Marie Murphy

Rachel D'Avino

Lauren Rousseau

the heroic teachers who were massacred while trying to protect the beautiful children at Sandy Hook Elementary School and whose deaths defy all principles of common sense in our morality, humanity, and laws.

Contents

About the Author

Ken Tanner began his career scrubbing dishes in the back of a Pizza Hut, eventually becoming the youngest manager in that chain's history. What followed was a 20-year career in the hospitality industry that included management of hotels, owning a dinner theater, and serving as a regional vice president for two of the nation's biggest restaurant chains. That phase of his career featured dramatic customer service turnarounds, record low employee turnover rates, and the development of dozens of industry leaders. Ken is especially proud of the number of women he helped advance into executive positions.

Ken founded a human resources consulting firm in 1995. Initially focused on recruiting, he now uses his expertise to help companies retain employees and help Boomers build their careers. Ken is proud to be the lowest ranking elected official in the state of Georgia. He is the author of five other business books on team building and careers, including *Recruiting Excellence, Never Order Barbecue in Maine*, and *The Boomers' Career Survival Guide*. Ken can be reached at kentanner@consultant.com.

Acknowledgments

I am grateful to so many people who contributed to the production of this book. Here is an incomplete list of those who honored me with their thoughts and examples:

My friends at E. Quinn, Bookseller, Blue Ridge, Georgia, for their wonderful contributions of commonsense sayings. This is a bookstore the way bookstores ought to be.

My daughter Katherine, for giving me insight into how an American teenager processes logic.

My editor, Jeff Olson. I hope the finished product does some honor to his amazing patience, integrity, and talent. I treasure his friendship.

The Chick-Fil-A Eastlake, Biscuits and More of Marietta, Georgia, and Panera Bread at the Avenue of East Cobb, for letting me take up their tables for hours at a time while writing this book.

And to the many people who have contributed their perspectives. This incomplete list includes Heather Howard; Gary Barnett; David Roddy; Pete Van Weiren; Sir Edmund Hillary; Blanch Tosh; Dale Naftzger; Senators Howard Baker, Bill Brock, and Lamar Alexander; Dr. James Hatley; Almeda Hooper; Sam Battistone; John Lewis; Andrew Young; Melissa Russell; Evelyn Wood; Dr. Michael DeBakey; Dawn Wells; Dr. Jim Jenson; Shar Childers; Troy Waugh; Jerry Nichols; Fred Scarpace; Ralph Reed; Clint Clark; Michelle Moberg; Neil Armstrong; Bryant Wright; Dale Murphy; Dr. Yasser Jabri; Sam Olens; Mary Stephens; James Brady; Msquared; Peggy Noonan; Howard Singer; Nick Davis; Jorje Meistra; and hundreds of other friends and acquaintances who made great contributions to my understanding of common sense.

Special thanks to the many people who blatantly displayed an incredible lack of common sense. Discretion (and potential libel lawsuits) require me to omit their names.[1]

And, oh yes, thanks to my wife, Montine, for saving my life twice during the writing of this book. I appreciate it.

---

[1] Except for four politicians I do name. Their being public figures gets me around the libel thingie.

Preface

Caution! Genius at Work

The courtroom was hushed as the defense attorney rose to make his closing statement. Although the case presented some tough challenges for the prosecution—after all, the police had never actually found a body—the evidence did seem to point convincingly to the absolute fact that the defendant did indeed kill his wife. Not only was there no reasonable doubt, there seemed to be no doubt.

But the folks in the courtroom had perhaps underestimated the skills of Basil Simmons, the Harvard–educated New York lawyer who then rose to speak. Simmons looked at the jury and announced, "I agree with the prosecutor that the evidence looks rather convincing. If I were in your shoes, I'd be pretty impressed with some of the facts presented." The jury, the gallery, and even the judge nodded their heads in agreement with this statement. "But there is one important thing missing from the prosecutor's case. The fact is, my client's wife is still alive!"

Well, that would certainly change things, the jurors seemed to be thinking. Simmons continued: "And to prove that she is still alive, in thirty seconds Mrs. Randall will walk right through that door! Eyes in the jury box looked at the doorway. Simmons held his dramatic pose, pointing at the door for a full 30 seconds as everyone seemed to hold their breath. As the seconds ticked away, all eyes shifted from the empty door back to Simmons. He continued with his dramatic statement. "No, Mrs. Randall did not walk through that door, but you all were looking and expecting her to. We call that 'reasonable doubt.' And because you have demonstrated you have reasonable doubt, you must use your common sense and find my client not guilty!"

After an unusually short deliberation, the jury announced their verdict: guilty. The courtroom was stunned, but no one more so than the defense attorney. He rushed up to the jury foreman and challenged, "How could you find him guilty? You were supposed to use your common sense!"

"We did use our common sense," replied the foreman. "That's why we found him guilty."

"But, I proved reasonable doubt! Admit it, you all looked at that doorway!"

"Yeah, we looked," admitted the foreman. "But your client didn't."

Common Sense: Not So Uncommon

When I mentioned to friends I was writing a book about common sense, I received dozens of replies quoting Voltaire: Common sense is not so common. The fact this was the immediate response from so many underscores the perception that the world is sadly lacking in common sense.

Although I fear bucking the perception held by most of the world, I respectfully disagree with Voltaire. Common sense is actually quite common. We just don't perceive it that way for a couple of reasons.

First, we tend to worship those who have formal institutional knowledge and put them on a high pedestal. We even give them grand titles or credentials such as Doctor, MBA, PhD, or even The Honorable. Furthermore, we almost mock those with folk knowledge. Example? Just about the wisest character I know is Sheriff Andy Taylor on *The Andy Griffith Show*. He solves problems and leads through common sense; yet, to most casual observers, he appears to be a dull country bumpkin (as most of us Southerners seem to be perceived by the North). Despite barely having a high school education, Andy regularly outsmarts the crack criminologists from Raleigh by applying some basic common sense. But have you noticed that a show in which common sense trumps book knowledge is referred to as a comedy? A show in which traditional education conquers the demons is usually a heavy drama. Hmmm.

Another reason we perceive common sense to be in short supply is because common sense is often what we have and our opponents don't. It's a great term to use for ending an argument or for supporting any argument that we don't otherwise have any real facts to support. "Of course the country ought to adopt this new law, it's just common sense!" Because we use that argument so often, it tends to label any intellectual opponent as lacking in common sense. Thus, we believe there is little common sense in the world, but most of it is possessed by only ourselves and those who agree with us.

I developed this book because I wanted to explore this often tossed-about term and to bring some concreteness to the concept. I also wanted to share my findings with you, so you could learn to apply common sense to situations that arise—especially at work—and look like a genius in the process. The first step in writing any book is to discover what similar titles may be on the market, which ones are successful, and which crashed and burned. For instance, when writing *The Boomers' Career Survival Guide*,[1] I found hundreds of books about career development, how to deal with life crises, and the psychological characteristics of my generation; likewise with books I've written about recruiting and team building, I found the market flooded with titles attempting to analyze the topics from an original new angle.

A funny thing happened, though, when I did my common sense survey. Although a search of the term *common sense* pulled up hundreds of titles, not one of them was *about* common sense. Let me explain. Books with common sense in the title seemed to use the term to say, "Here is some common sense about this topic." For instance, a book titled *Common Sense in Foreign* Policy was not about common sense; it was about politics. Likewise *Common Sense in the Church*, *Common Sense in the Classroom*, or *Common Sense for Lawyers*[2] were about religion, education, or the legal system. The use of the term common sense was just for effect; it was the authors way of saying: Here is a lot of obvious stuff. So, despite the seemingly importance of common sense, no one had really tried to tackle the topic itself! Thus the creation of this book.

Help Wanted: People with Common Sense

As a former recruiter and headhunter, I have written extensively on the subject of careers. My best research comes from interviewing successful people and business leaders. I always ask these folks to list the traits they most desire in their employees. A long languid litany of skills, personal qualities, and talents always follows, but inevitably three things float to the top: leadership, teamwork, and common sense.

Here are some facts my research confirmed: Executives want to hire people with good common sense. Common sense will enhance your performance exponentially. Common sense will provide you with an incredible competitive advantage. Quite simply, common sense will propel your career.

It was obvious common sense was a critical career commodity, but a question begged to be asked: Is a person born with common sense or is it something that can be learned?

---

[1] Yes, this is, indeed, a shameless self-promotion.
[2] Candidate for oxymoron of the year?

Let me pull out my industrial psychologist hat for a moment and explain why some people perceive common sense to be genetic. You may have noticed people with common sense tend to have parents with common sense, thus the conclusion that it is something in the DNA. However, I believe the phenomenon occurs because the parents teach the child, through constant life and situational examples, how to use common sense—kind of an 18-year training program.

Common Sense Can Be Learned, and Taught

So I have some good news for you: Common sense can be learned, it can be developed, and it can be taught. This book is devoted to doing just these things. I'll show you how to develop common sense in your employees as well as enhance the common sense you already have in your personal portfolio.

Let me make an important point about developing people. I've always espoused that the best way to learn how to do something right is to learn how to stop doing things wrong. I devote much of this instruction to examining "common nonsense" actions—how to recognize them, correct them, and avoid them. We'll also have a little fun looking at some big examples of common nonsense we see in our daily lives, with a glimpse at the ultimate common nonsense broadcaster: the Internet.

We'll also examine how to use common sense to make decisions, how to apply this critical tool to business, and how teach your employees to use good common sense. In short, we're going to look at how to recognize, use, and teach common sense in your business and career.

But perhaps the overriding question right now is: Just what in the heck is common sense? In the current lexicon, common sense may be an ambiguous term, like kindness or honesty or righteousness. In other words, common sense is in the eye of the beholder. Or better yet, common sense is simply whatever my opinion is. But, rather than ramble through a lot of fluff, let's put some tangible definition to the term. Before we learn all about how to acquire, use, and teach common sense, let's first turn the page and decide what it is.

That, after all, is just common sense.

What Is Common Sense, Anyway?

If left to the U.S. Supreme Court, the term *common sense* would probably be labeled in the same manner dirty pictures were defined. When asked what constituted pornography, one esteemed jurist noted, "I'll know it when I see it." We generally can identify common sense when we see it. Perhaps more important, we find it quite easy to identify when we *don't* see it. A lack of common sense can be easily spotted when you hear an excited voice bark, pointing it out, *What in the world were you thinking‽*[1]

Often, the term is used defensively or as a way to get the final word in an argument. "Of course I'm right," we'll say. "After all, it's just common sense."

I once judged a high school debate during which a young lady was clearly overmatched by a prep school genius with an impeccable command of the facts. Her opponent seemed to be the clear winner until, in a critical analysis of terminology, he issued what should have been the *coup de grace*

---

[1] You hold history in your hands. As best we can determine, this is the first book to use an *interebang*—‽—since 1966.

by saying "Webster defines [xxx] as . . . ." To which the novice replied, "Who is Webster to decide what a word means?" I gave her the victory.

Although I do not grant Mr. Webster the right to deliver the definitive bottom line on the definition, I must admit he delivers a pretty good summary of common sense:

> Beliefs or propositions that most people consider prudent and of sound judgment, without reliance on esoteric knowledge or study or research, but based upon what they see as knowledge held by people in common.

Whew. Let me put that into a more digestible language: *Common sense is the ability to think logically without using specialized or advanced knowledge.*

Perhaps the best way to understand the nature of common sense (CS) is to study it in action. I've noticed that all discussions of common sense tend to compare, contrast, or combine it with knowledge gained through formal study. Let's examine common sense—or lack thereof—alongside its close cousin: formal education.

Two factors determine our judgment and decision-making capacity. The first is the target of this book: common sense. The other is what people traditionally measure when evaluating how smart someone is: knowledge developed through formal education or training. Formal education, such as college, trade school, company training programs, workshops, independent study, and so forth, will be referred to by the term *book smarts*, or BS for short.

There are four possible ways to combine these two judgment-determining factors. Let's look at these combinations and see the probable results in the lives and actions of those holding the combinations. We'll begin with the most unfortunate combination, a person having neither formal education nor common sense.

Common sense   Never order barbecue in Maine.

–CS –BS (Low Common Sense, Low Book Smarts)

My cousin Ralph was working with the new kid in his construction company. They were installing planks on the side of a home they were building. Cousin Ralph glanced at his apprentice and noticed a peculiar behavior.

Judson would hammer in a nail, then reach into his satchel, take out another nail, shake his head with disgust, then throw the nail to the ground. He continued doing this, discarding every other nail, for about half an hour before Ralph decided to question the novice's strange actions.

"Them nails is defective," Judson explained. "About half of 'em have the point on the wrong end."

Ralph rolled his eyes, sighed, and decided to make it a teaching moment. "Damn, boy! Are you stupid? Those nails are for the *other* side of the house."

At first glance, this combination of intelligences (or lack thereof) would seem to be a humor generator. And in fiction or the movies, it certainly is. Think of the Three Stooges, Jerry Lewis characters, or the entire cast of *Dumb and Dumber*.[2] Characters lacking in both education and common sense are prime fodder for great jokes and silliness. In fact, if you study the construction of humor, you will note that the funny characters over-whelmingly have this unfortunate combination of low traits.

Although it plays well in fiction, in real life this combination doesn't gener-ate anything to smile about. The −CS −BS class is heavily populated by the criminal and antisocial mind. In fact, our prisons are filled with people pos-sessing this pathetic combination of −CS −BS. Here are some examples from around the world:

- Tampa, Florida: A robber was arrested after police were called by a taxi driver—the one she asked to wait for her while she went in to rob a store.

- Detroit, Michigan: A woman was arrested when she complained to police that she had not received deliv-ery of the marijuana she paid for.

- Fargo, North Dakota: A −CS −BS bank robber scrib-bled his ransom note and gave it to the teller. She gave him the money and watched him run out the door. When reviewing the ransom note, it was dis-covered that the man wrote the ransom note on his personal bank deposit slip.

- Chattanooga, Tennessee: A man barged into a drug store, waved a pistol, and pulled a Hefty bag facemask over his head. He then realized he had forgotten to cut eyeholes in his mask.

---

[2]And its brilliantly titled sequel, *Dumb and Dumberer*.

- Rouen, France: Moments after robbing a bank, a man jumped into a car, ordering that the driver, "Get away quick, before the cops come!" He didn't notice that the car he was hijacking was a police car.

- Los Angeles, California: When detectives asked each man in the lineup to repeat the words: "Give me all your money or I'll shoot," one man shouted, "That's not what I said!"

- Honolulu, Hawaii: When a detective informed him he was suspected of robbing four banks, the criminal retorted, "I didn't do four; I only robbed three banks."

- Colorado Springs, Colorado: Waving a shotgun, a rookie robber demanded the contents of the cash register. The cashier promptly complied, but then the robber spotted a bottle of scotch. He ordered the cashier also to give him the bottle, but the cashier refused. "I don't believe you are over 21," the clerk explained. The robber pulled out his driver's license and handed it to the clerk. The clerk agreed that the man was, indeed, of legal age, so he added the scotch to the bag of loot. The police later arrested the robber at the address the cashier got from his license.

- Richmond, Virginia: A robber cleverly hid his identity by pulling a ski mask over his face. Unfortunately, he was wearing his work uniform, which had the name of his company as well as his name stitched across the front.

- Barcelona, Spain: A man and woman were hiding items in their bags and clothing and fled when the store manager spotted them. They were in such a hurry that they left behind a stroller containing their baby. The couple was arrested when they returned to the store later in the day to ask about their infant.

- Boulder, Colorado: Sometimes you can use common sense to defeat those totally void of it. Our +CS hero was shocked to find her bicycle had been stolen. She looked on Craigslist to see if the thief was stupid enough to place it there for sale. Yep; he was. So she visited the seller and he agreed she could take a test ride. And she promptly stole the bike back.

As police detective Jorge Mestre says, "Never underestimate the ignorance of a criminal." The point is made. –CS –BS is a most unfortunate
combination to possess.

Common sense   "Laugh at yourself first before anyone else can." —Elsa Maxwell

---

–CS +BS (Low Common Sense, High Book Smarts)

There is a Persian proverb that notes: *One pound of learning requires ten
pounds of common sense to apply it.* This saying is well expressed in one of
today's premier cartoons, DILBERT. In one set of panels, the pointy-hair
boss is interviewing an applicant and is quite impressed with his long
list of graduate degrees. The applicant humbly replies, "Yes, but interestingly I have no common sense whatsoever." When the boss points out it's
probably not a good idea to mention this in a job interview, the genius
responds, "I don't see why not."

People possessing –CS +BS have amassed excellent education and training, but enjoy a low level of basic common sense. Although the stereotype
caricature for this category is the "nutty professor," many politicians do
fit nicely into this category. Dennis Kucinich, Ron Paul, Nancy Pelosi, and
Newt Gingrich float immediately to the surface. There is no doubt these
folks are smart and well educated—in fact, two of them hold doctoral
degrees! I stand in awe of the depth of their intellect. But, regardless
of your political persuasion, you gotta shake your head with embarrass-
ment when you hear some of the common nonsense these politicians
generate.[3]

Here's one of my favorite examples of –CS +BS. During one 2000 presidential debate, Al Gore explained a bold plan for enhancing the nation's
education standards. Schools would be evaluated to ensure their quality
and effectiveness. Dramatic action would be taken if a school fell below
the required level of excellence and showed no dependable improvement.
In fact, if they failed on a Friday, every single teacher would be fired and
replaced on Monday morning. And they would not be replaced by just *any*
teachers; they would be replaced by the highest quality teachers America

---

[3]OK, I know I'm treading on thin ice here, but work with me. Notice the point I'm
making and forgive me for stepping on political toes.

had to offer. Thus, the problem schools would be fixed immediately and decisively.

This brilliant proposal drew enthusiastic applause and cheers. It did seem symbolic of Gore's ability to analyze a problem, garner the needed resources, and take dynamic action. Although it was, indeed, brilliant, basic common sense was lacking. How's that? Well, you know all those incredible teachers who were going to show up Monday morning—where were they Friday afternoon? Were they sitting at home, unpaid, just hoping for the phone to ring, telling them a school full of teachers needed replacing and they had a job next week? And if these teachers were "the best," why didn't they already have teaching jobs? Or perhaps Gore would have already hired them and paid them to be on standby. But why would we hire brilliant teachers and have them sit on the bench "just in case?"

Another case of −CS +BS also involves Albert Gore, but this time he is not the perpetrator. Instead, the culprit is the oft-in-the-news Transportation Security Administration (TSA). During its early years, the fledgling TSA began experimenting with new airline security procedures. These initial procedures included random security inspections at the gate. Although routine today (now, *everyone* has to remove their shoes), at that time, only one or two haphazardly selected passengers would have their feet screened for weapons and bombs. On one particular flight, from more than two hundred passengers, the TSA selected former Vice President Albert Gore for closer scrutiny. I am no fan of Albert Gore; however, I will wager my left arm and the family farm that there is zero chance Vice President Gore was planning to hijack that airplane.

Why was Gore selected for this honor? I guess the TSA wanted to prove they didn't use racial profiling. Personally, I'd rather they would prove they are ensuring airline safety. Political correctness may be the ultimate rejection of common sense.

Another example of −CS +BS comes to us courtesy of the tobacco industry.[4] A frantic meeting was once held by a company's marketing department to analyze the failure of a highly touted new product. To cash in on the "organic" consumer trend, tens of millions of dollars had been spent to develop a brand using all-natural ingredients and organic farming procedures. Despite their diligent research, the product completely bombed.

The executives—the most educated and experienced minds in American industry—were tossing the blame around the table, astutely analyzing what the other guy did wrong. Then, a young intern sheepishly spoke up.

---

[4]Perhaps the very existence of the tobacco industry could be considered a metaphor for the dearth of common sense.

"I'm thinking people who are into organic products don't smoke cigarettes," she reasoned.

Although −CS +BS can sometimes generate good ideas, if the common sense factor is too low, it can lead to some rather embarrassing results.

Common sense   A closed mouth gathers no foot.

+CS −BS (High Common Sense, Low Book Smarts)

My dear Uncle Alfred holds an impressive position at the Centers for Disease Control and Prevention (CDC). He is in charge of a group of scientists who brainstorm ways to combat diseases that have confounded the greatest minds of our generation. Al didn't get this job through any traditional route. He doesn't have a medical degree, a doctorate of chemistry, or even an engineering pedigree. In fact, he barely squeaked out his high school diploma. Here is how it happened. Uncle Alfred was a maintenance man at the CDC. One day, he was changing the air filters in a conference room where some esteemed scientists were struggling with the problem of West Nile Virus. "Excuse me," he interrupted, "but why don't we just do whatever the people in East Nile do?"

Sometimes knowledge can become an intellectual barrier. I have a trivia question that serves me well in stumping the most knowledgeable baseball gurus. It is: *Of all the players who have retired wearing a Braves uniform, who has the most career homeruns?* I put this question to the ultimate test by presenting it to Pete van Wieren. Pete was an Atlanta Braves announcer for 30 years and was nicknamed *The Professor* for his amazing encyclopedic knowledge of baseball statistics. If anyone knew a Braves record, it would be him. His answer? "Hank Aaron, of course." I reminded him that Aaron retired wearing a Brewers uniform. "Oh, I see," he replied. "Then it wouldn't be Dale Murphy either." His mind worked for several minutes longer; I could almost see statistics reflected in his eyeballs. And then he uttered the words I never thought I'd hear from The Professor's lips: "I don't know. You stumped me."

Why didn't Pete get the obvious answer to my trivia question? *Because he knew too much.* His immediate reaction was clouded by the need to search his mental archives for what was assumed to be an obscure statistic. It seems all baseball fans who are known for their deep knowledge of stats do this. They overlook the obvious. So is it any surprise that the *only* person who has answered this question correctly was a lady with casual baseball familiarity but tons of rational ability? When I asked Shar Childers, "Of all the players who have retired wearing a Braves uniform, who had the most career homeruns?" she replied, "Babe Ruth."

Sometimes we just think too hard.

+CS +BS (High Common Sense, High Book Smarts)

Now +CS +BS this is the best possible combination. A deep level of common sense combined with a powerful education or highly specialized training can deliver not only excellent results, but also creative ones as well. Consider some of the sparkling examples of this pairing from the past century: Mark Twain, Franklin Roosevelt, and Winston Churchill.

The first organization that comes to mind when looking for an example of possessing both extraordinary book smarts and solid common sense is the U.S. Secret Service.[5] The most visible responsibility this group is charged with is the protection of the president. One way they must do this is to ensure the food in the First Family's kitchen is safe and has not been poisoned by some sinister operative. How do they do this?

The immediate thought is to set up sophisticated systems to inspect closely the food being delivered to the White House, analyzing it chemically to confirm it is not poisoned. Furthermore, using their highly developed investigative techniques, the Secret Service could explore the lives of all suppliers, verifying no one in their companies has any hint of a terrorist connection. A complex procedure could certainly be designed to make sure the food entering the president's kitchen is not touched by anything harmful.

But, despite their ability to produce such a system, this is not how the Secret Service ensures no one poisons the president's groceries. Instead, it simply selects a supermarket at random, moments before a couple of agents go grocery shopping. If a bad guy wants to poison the first family, he'll have to poison all the food in every grocery store within a hundred miles of Washington.

---

[5] This section was written before the headlines of the Colombian hooker scandal, in which many of the Secret Service members assigned to guard the president in Cartagena apparently had prostitutes in their hotel room, which proves that even people with great common sense often don't use it.

Sometimes common sense trumps book smarts, even when the person has enormous book smarts.

Perhaps the biggest headline of our generation is the miraculous advances in medicine. Millions of people are alive, living great lives, despite chronic diseases that would have been a death sentence just 20 years ago. Imagine the progress over the next 20 years; it will be exponential.

Here is a wonderful example of this continuing miracle. Consider the treatment of heart failure, the heart transplant, and the artificial heart. We have already witnessed staggering progress in heart care. Transplants, which 30 years ago made world headlines, are now an almost-routine procedure at many hospitals. But, despite the amazing advancements in transplants, their use has been limited by the number of donor hearts available—thus the need for artificial organs. This technology faces a serious roadblock, however. Although an artificial heart can be made that works pretty well initially, it is a tool with standards that rival perfection. A heart beats more than 2.5 million times a month, and no one has been able to build a machine that can take that kind of action without regular adjustments and repair. No matter how brilliant the scientists, doctors, and engineers have been, not one has been able to figure out how to go in there and squirt some WD-40 from time to time or how to replace the tiny parts that tend to wear out after just a few million beats. And although we can build equipment that works great most of the time, this standard is just not good enough when dealing with a heart. You see, if a car breaks down for 15 minutes every 6 months, no problem. In fact, this would be an outstanding, quality performance. But if a heart has the same failure rate, the patient is dead.

Then one day, a +CS +BS scientist took a step back and rethought the situation. He noted that when Wilber and Orville invented the airplane, they didn't imitate nature. The wings on the Wright flyer didn't flap like a bird; they found a different way to create lift. So, if the airplane didn't duplicate nature's solution, why should the heart? The only reason artificial hearts were made to beat was because this is the way nature chose to address the problem of circulation.

The +CS +BS scientist realized the goal was not to produce a machine that beat, *it was to produce a machine that circulated blood.* Although a dependable heartbeat is impossible to produce, a continuously flowing pump is, mechanically, the simplest—and most error-free—machine to maintain.[6]

---

[6]http://minnesota.publicradio.org/display/web/2013/01/09/daily-circuit-pumpless-heart?refid=0

Thus, the next generation of artificial hearts will be continuous-flowing systems. This innovation may soon make heart disease a routinely managed, chronic condition—a true miracle brought about by combining distinguished education with plain old common sense.

■ **Common sense** "I never thought I didn't have a card to play." —*Apollo 13* Commander Jim Lovell

---

Summary

In the world of intellect, there is strong parallel between folk art and common sense. Folk art is defined as works created by self-taught artists, those who have no formal training. Common sense is similar; it is the product of a person using no specialized education or training in the subject being analyzed. Just as folk art is as rich as any produced by formally trained artists, good commonsense decisions carry the same credibility of many produced by Nobel laureates.

Although this book focuses on how to develop and teach common sense, let's first pause and look at methods to create the image of common sense and, also, how to avoid using the opposite trait: common nonsense.

After all this analysis and dissection, perhaps we can leave it to Ralph Waldo Emerson to capture the true definition of common sense: "Common sense is genius dressed in its working clothes." This definition will serve us quite nicely as we proceed.

Perception Is Reality

Everyone wants to increase their common sense, right? Of course! But maybe more important than increasing your actual common sense is to increase the *perception* of your having it.

To illustrate the importance perception is to having an image of good common sense, let's look at two examples from our history book. Two men—both with well-above-average IQs—made public mistakes, yet one was glossed over and the other almost vilified by it.

The first man was President John F. Kennedy. While standing in front of the Berlin Wall in 1963, the president wanted to inspire the crowd of one million West Germans in his speech. He wanted to let them know in their own language that he was one of them and would be proud to declare "I am a Berliner!" So, in a dramatic voice, he announced, "Ich bin ein Berliner!" The inspired crowd roared its approval. Never mind that what Kennedy had actually said was, "I am a jelly donut."

Fast forward 30 years to the case of Vice President Dan Quayle. Making an appearance at an elementary school spelling bee, he declared that potato was actually spelled with an "e" on the end. The ridicule heaped on Quayle took on a life of its own, and the late-night talk show hosts teased Quayle endlessly for this rather elementary mistake. But there is a bit more to this story. You see, the card the vice president was reading from stated p-o-t-a-t-o-e. And his aides, who had previewed the card deck prior to his appearance (to avoid this very fiasco) had assured him that all the words in the deck were correct.

Now, I'm not declaring these situations are equal in any way. Making a speech before a million enslaved people is far more consequential than a fifth-grade spelling bee. But this may be the point. Because of the significance of the event, Kennedy's error posed the danger of much greater ridicule. However, while Kennedy had built a perception of eloquence and competence over the course of a decade, Quayle kept stumbling into embarrassing situations that generated the perception that he lacked basic common sense.

The reality is that both men had (and have, in the case of Quayle) great common sense. But, because of the perception that Quayle is sadly lacking in this department, any error he makes is labeled as the ongoing product of a dullard.

Common sense   Everyone has a spark of genius; some people simply have ignition problems.

Ensure Others Perceive You as Having Common Sense

The perception of common sense—or lack thereof—is as powerful as actually possessing the trait. So how do you avoid developing a reputation for deficient common sense? Perhaps the best way is to master some basic knowledge about life. No, I'm not talking about mastering Eastern philosophy or engineering a rocket; instead, I'm referring to some fundamental things. The fact is, there are some essentials a human being just ought to know or know how to do. Lacking these skills and abilities will make sure others perceive you as not having any common sense.

What follows is a list that will ensure you impress others with your perspicacity. This is not, of course, an all-inclusive list, but it should get you well on your way to avoiding the label of a person who is commonsense deficient.

Be Computer Literate

Much as I would like to think computers are a passing fad like fax machines, I've about come to the conclusion they are now a staple of life. Early in my career, being computer literate was a sign of genius. Today, computer literacy is as necessary as knowing how to tie your shoes. If you can't tie your shoes, you are labeled as having no common sense—the same with an inability to operate a computer.

When I say computer literate, I don't mean you must be able to program or operate sophisticated software. No. Just be able to use the Internet, go to Google for information you need, and use simple word processing and spreadsheet applications. And don't limit yourself to just the computer. There are other office machines, such as the fancy copier that can send documents to computers worldwide, and the coffee pot, that require you to possess a working knowledge of basic technology. These skills are nothing special, but lacking them gets you labeled in unflattering terms.

Cook Simple Items

You don't have to qualify as a four-star chef—just be able to prepare some simple staples. Preparing spaghetti, scrambled eggs, pancakes, grilled chicken, rice, and a burger must be in your repertoire. And make sure you can make a pot of coffee and, if you live in the South, brew a pitcher of iced tea.

You can take this a step further by learning how to take prepared foods and add items to them to make it look like you are a gourmet chef. For instance, take a frozen lasagna and add extra meat, peppers, cheese, and sauce. You will amaze your friends with your culinary abilities and banish any accusation that you don't have enough sense to boil water.

Perform Basic First Aid

Nothing fancy here—although it *is* a good idea to learn CPR—just the ability to attend to some of the everyday boo-boos that invade our lives. Know to put a minor burn under cold running water. Rinse out a wound before bandaging it. Apply pressure to a bleeding injury to make the blood stop flowing. And never give a glass of water to someone who is having a seizure. I urge you to take a basic first-aid course through the Red Cross so you won't panic when people need your help.

And make sure you know the phone number to your local 911 bureau.

Tip   Learn first aid so you can help people in need and—nearly as important—so you don't freak out under pressure.

Perform Routine Home Maintenance

I know of a philosophy professor at the University of Chicago who had no idea how to change a light bulb. (In fact, he was not even aware that they could be changed.) If this multidegreed person is stumped by such a task, perhaps there are many others who cannot fix a leaky toilet, hang a picture, or operate a weed-eater. Some of these skills have an application at the office. Chances are, if you cannot maintain your home, you can't maintain your work area either.

Perform Routine Housework

Even if you are at the station in life when you can employ a full-time maid, you must be able to take care of your household. (After all, the maid gets a day off each week.) A possessor of common sense can wash dishes, sweep the floor, mop up a spill, operate the clothes dryer, iron a shirt, and make a bed. Again, these skills, or lack thereof, translate directly to your office or work area. An inability to complete basic domestic tasks not only makes you appear to have no common sense, it makes you a slob, which is not a socially acceptable combination.

Perform Basic Automobile Care

The TV show *Frasier* featured a pair of brothers—Frasier and Niles Crane—who were both brilliant psychiatrists but sometimes lacking in the world of practical knowledge. Perhaps this strong −CS +BS streak was most apparent when it came to dealing with their automobiles.

In one episode, the brothers were starting an auto trip when the engine would not start. "Should we look under the hood?" Frasier asks. "Won't that void the warranty?" Niles replies.

Avoid becoming a Crane brother. Know a few basic things about your car. Be able to jump-start a dead battery, check your tire pressure, pump your own gas, and change a flat tire. And—I pass this along via personal experience—it is critical that you regularly check the oil in your company car.

Shuffle a Deck of Cards

People who can't shuffle always lose. It's hard to bluff your way through a poker hand when you look like a loser before the cards are even dealt.[1]

---

[1] Astute readers will recognize this entry is not about shuffling cards, but is a metaphor for preparation in general.

▓ **Common sense**   Borrow money from pessimists; they don't expect to get it back.

Know the Basic Rules of the Major Sports

You don't need to be an über-fan, simply be able to listen to a conversation about baseball, football, or basketball without having a blank look on your face. Know how points are scored, what the different positions do, and who the big-name teams and athletes are. Be aware of the reigning champions of the World Series, the Superbowl, and the NBA Championships. (The World Cup? Not so much.) In our sports-crazed society, not knowing that a field goal is worth three points will not only get you branded as lacking common sense, some people will think you are a subversive communist.

Relate Statistics Logically

My uncle Alfred teamed up with his neighbor and they went on their first fishing trip. Not knowing exactly what to expect, they first stopped at a sporting goods store to buy the proper equipment. The salesman must have seen them coming, because he was able to unload every item that could possibly be related to catching a fish.

With their Jeep fully loaded with gear, my uncle and his friend headed to a nearby lake, rented a cabin for three days, and set up their enterprise. On the first day, they sat for hours without even so much as a nibble. Day two, same story. Finally, on day three, Neptune tossed them a bone and Alfred hauled in a scrappy little crappie. They then sat there for a few more hours before calling it a day.

As they were packing up their extensive gear, Alfred noted that the trip had cost them $1,500 per fish. "Sure am glad we didn't catch any more fish than that," his friend replied. "I'd go broke."

Statistically, my uncle's friend was correct, but it is not a very big exaggeration from how many people use statistics. A childhood friend once posed this logic question to me: if it takes a ship seven days to cross the ocean, does it take seven ships one day to cross? He was just being clever, of course, but it is amazing how many people, included learned statesmen, can play with numbers to make them mean pretty much the opposite of what they actually do mean.

Don't do this. Intentional or not, twisted statistics—although you may get away with it for a moment—are eventually discovered by the victim. And then you look really stupid.[2]

Take Care of Yourself Without Being Nagged

This statement is directed at the men reading this paragraph. (Women really don't have this deficiency, which is probably the reason women live about seven years longer than we do.) For some reason, we men think that if we ignore something, it will go away. The fact is, it usually does. But when it doesn't, it will jump up and bite us on the caboose. Although we seem to understand the need to maintain our automobiles, we are lost when applying that same logic to our own body. Eventually, we all come down with something that kills us. (The human mortality rate is a verifiable 100%.) However, it's a shame when we catch some disease that takes us out 30 years early all because we didn't have the common sense to check out that funny looking mole, monitor our blood pressure, or take a baby aspirin daily.

Remember Names

Sherlock was telling me of a system he had learned at a recent workshop. "The instructor was fantastic!" he said. "He taught us simply to associate the person's name with an object."

"That's interesting," I said. "Who was the instructor?"

Sherlock's eyes lit up as he recognized the challenge I had laid before him. "OK, let's see. What is that flower that comes in all sorts of colors and you give it to your wife on anniversaries?"

"Rose?" I guessed.

"Yeah, that's it, *Rose*. Then he turned and called over his shoulder, "Rose, honey, what was the name of that instructor?"

Find a system that works for you; being able to recall someone's name makes a marked difference in their perception of you. And use it often in conversation. As Dale Carnegie pointed out, "Remember that a person's name is, to that person, the sweetest and most important sound in any language."

---

[2]Here's my favorite statistic: 83.79% of all statistics are made up on the spot.

Don't Overthink

Sometimes we feel the need to consider all possibilities before making a decision. Although this can be a good personal policy to possess for long-term planning, it can get you into real trouble when you need to make quick decisions.

The invisible angels manning the phones at your local 911 bureau must make important—often lifesaving—decisions and they must do it quickly. When a caller contacts them with a medical emergency, the operator must diagnose the issue within seconds so she can send the proper equipment and provide critical care instructions. Most medical emergencies are complicated, and symptoms can be analyzed from countless angles, but doing so takes precious seconds away from the dispatch. Operators avoid fatal overanalysis by remembering this old saying from their training: if you hear hoofbeats, it very well could be a zebra, but it is probably a horse.

But Don't Underthink Either

In an earlier life, I served as a regional vice president for a couple of fast-food companies. My team made enormous improvements in customer service, much caused through our obsession with listening to the customer. I set the example on this by reading and responding to every single card left in any of the 100+ restaurants in my region.

I learned much from this feedback but must admit I was occasionally befuddled. My most unusual case of someone missing the point he was trying to make was this one:

While preparing my food, the cook scratched his face and then proceeded to make my sandwich. Yuck! I think your people ought to wear gloves.

Really. He is disgusted with ickies transferred from face to food by hands, but not by gloves?

Not to leave you hanging on this issue, but here is the real story on the use of gloves by food workers. As you realize, it is not hands that are unsanitary, it is the things hands touch. A major restaurant company did research on glove use, taking regular samples for bacteria from both gloved hands and bare hands. To no one's surprise, gloved hands were tremendously filthier than bare hands. Why was this? It's because people using bare hands can feel the ickies and tend to wash their hands regularly.

Those wearing gloves, however, have a sense of invulnerability, cannot feel their hands getting dirty, and rarely wash or change the gloves.

I recently had another encounter with this demonstration of missing the point. Interestingly, it also involved gloves. (This is becoming a metaphor.) I was in the hospital and was about to undergo a procedure requiring absolute sanitation. It was not a common procedure, so the head nurse was demonstrating to a class of nurses how to perform it. She emphasized the critical need for sanitation and had all of them wash their hands thoroughly before donning masks and gloves. Then, as she was about to hook me up to the machine, her phone rang. She didn't hesitate and reached down, pulled her cell phone off her belt, and had her conversation. She hung up, placed the phone back on her belt, and then reached to make the connection. "No!" I barked diplomatically. "You are not sterile since you touched the phone." The nurse recoiled a bit, possibly embarrassed that I had corrected her in front of her subordinates. "No, I'm good," she explained. "I am wearing gloves."

Before declaring an obvious solution to a problem, take a step back and think about it briefly. Are you solving the problem or just slapping a glove on it?

Oppose Major League Baseball's Designated Hitter Rule

What does this have to do with common sense? Not a whole lot, except the designated hitter just isn't rational. Supporting it puts you on the wrong side of logic and could stall your career progression. Seriously. Would you promote someone who showed such a dearth of common sense?

Know Basic History

Again, no PhD is needed, but it is surprising how many otherwise smart people are lost on some of the basic facts of history. And I do mean basic. Be aware that World War I, preceded World War II, that Lincoln and Washington were not contemporaries, and that Ben Franklin was never president. Know a bit about Napoleon, Stalin, and Julius Caesar, too. If you really don't know history and a conversation erupts involving it, it is to your advantage to remain silent.[3]

Understand Government Economics

I know what you are thinking. *Nobody in government understands government economics, so why should I?* Actually, that is the very reason you should understand, lest you be labeled as lacking in common sense just like our Congress members. Don't dive deeply into Keynesian theory, just grasp a couple of commonsense economic principles, such as: If the government champions a new project, the money has to come from somewhere. Or, there really is no such thing as taxing corporations. (It's just a business expense passed along to the customer.) Or, if the government prints more money, the value of the individual bill is immediately devalued (well, eventually). Know these basic things. It's this lack of common sense that has the United States more than $16 trillion in debt.

Recognize Your Personal Alcohol Limits

This is far more than a commonsense issue; it can become a matter of life and death. Even if you do possess enough basic common sense not to get behind the wheel of a car after drinking, common sense requires you to identify where to draw the line other times, too. If you don't know your limits, you'll often display a complete lack of common sense in situations that could affect your relationships as well as your career. Alcohol can make you act silly on social occasions and say dumb things at business dinners. You don't have to be drunk as a skunk before creating an image that you are completely void of common sense. Know where that line is.

Tip   Alcohol has ruined friendships, careers, and lives. Know your limits.

---

[3]Here's a bit of trivia you can use to give the perception that you know a lot about history. Historians recognize that the United States has had three great presidents: George Washington, Abraham Lincoln, and Franklin Roosevelt. Washington was first inaugurated in 1789. In 1861, 72 years later, Lincoln was inaugurated. And 72 years after that, in 1933, Roosevelt was sworn in. So it looks like every 72 years the United States gets a great president.

Be Polite to the Police

My friend Bubba was pulled over by a motorcycle cop. His first words to the officer were, "So where are the rest of the Village People?" Many folks approach law enforcement with comments just as self-destructive, although not as humorous. *Why aren't you out chasing real criminals?* is one of the most oft-used, self-destructive comments. Recognize that if you acknowledge an officer's authority, he will not feel obligated to prove it to you. Have a polite, honest, businesslike conversation with a police officer and you will run an excellent chance of seeing a positive outcome.

Rehearse Spontaneous Public Comments

Jerry Seinfeld tells of a poll asking people what scared them the most. Public speaking was ranked number one. Death was number two. That's right, death was in second place. He observes, "At a funeral, more people would rather be the corpse than deliver the eulogy."

You will be called on from time to time to say a few words in public. If the first word from your mouth is "Uhhhh" you will be marked as lacking in common sense. So go ahead and memorize a couple of toasts, just in case you are called to make one at the next wedding. Outline a prayer in case you are singled out at church. Know some things about all the topics that might pop up at your next convention or business meeting. And commit a couple of all-purpose anecdotes to memory. Do these things and you will avoid appearing to be a bumbler the next time you are called on to say a few words. Have some comments prepared before going into any setting in which it might be possible that you will be called on to speak. Although you have carefully prepared these remarks, to onlookers it will appear you spoke on the spur of the moment.

Don't Smoke

Besides the very real danger to your health, a person who smokes broadcasts an image that shouts, *This person possesses no common sense whatsoever!* Why does smoking create this image? Because there is absolutely no logical reason for smoking, and the consequences of doing so are extensive, including death. Smoking makes no sense whatsoever.

If you are unable to kick the habit and choose to continue to smoke, at least you should avoid smoking in public, which is tough to do these days. Most buildings are no-smoking zones, so you are even forbidden to smoke in your own private office, which forces you outside. Most smokers then cluster in groups just outside the main entrance to the building, on display to visitors, customers, and senior executives (the ones determining your future at the company). So now, not only are your displaying your lack of common sense, you are broadcasting it in the most public way possible. You are putting a spotlight on it—a double dose of no common sense. So, if you can't kick this habit, at least keep it in the closet. Not only will your life depend on this, but your career and reputation could as well.

Demonstrate Good Manners

Failing to show good manners will have you labeled a rube. I'm not talking about etiquette here; I'm talking about the basic manners you learned as a child. The rules haven't changed since kindergarten. OK. You may want to brush up on knowing which fork or water glass to grab. (The water glass always throws me off. I've just learned to wait until everyone else has grabbed theirs before reaching for mine.) Don't stress out trying to figure out how to behave in society. The trick is not to learn something new; it is simply to practice what you already know.

Being courteous, showing respect, and being deferential to guests and coworkers are all traits you want ascribed to you. If you lack these traits, you get pigeonholed as a buffoon.

Know Basic Geography

I was showing a new senior manager around the city to which he was being relocated. As we stood on the bluffs of downtown Memphis, we peered a full mile across the muddy river. The scene was straight off a postcard, as a riverboat steamed down the middle of the historic waters. "Wow," he exclaimed, "This is really something." He then looked up at me and inquired, "What's the name of this river?" I never changed my perception of this ignorant MBA.

Common sense   I prefer wicked over foolish. The wicked are occasionally not wicked.

Don't Misuse E-mail

E-mail can be an incredible business tool or the root of great folly. Here are some tips for steering clear of the latter.

Never use e-mail to avoid difficult conversations that should be held in person. This includes chastising your colleagues, reprimanding your employees, or breaking up with your romantic partner. This type of e-mail misuse is just plain cowardly.

Never push the Send button when you're angry. It's just too easy to fire back a reply when you are pissed. If an e-mail makes you mad, wait at least an hour before sending a response.

Never use the CC line as a weapon. Want to become the office pariah? Routinely "CC" your boss whenever you send a critical e-mail. Your colleagues will be resentful and will find effective ways to retaliate.

Never build your legacy in an e-mail. Never write anything in an e-mail you would not want to see on the front page of *USA Today*. Or on your boss's desk.

Know Current Events

You will forfeit any claim to common sense if you are unaware of current events—if you don't know who won the Oscar for Best Picture, if you are oblivious to the top issues in a presidential campaign, if you have a blank look on your face when someone mentions a hurricane that is about to hit New Orleans, if you don't know the winner of the World Series, or if you ask, "Who's that?" when you hear the names Lindsey Lohan and Kim Kardashian.

You do not need to have an expert understanding of every subject, just an awareness. For instance, football may hold no interest whatsoever, but if you do business in Indianapolis, you must be aware that its team is named the *Colts*. You should also know they have a hot new quarterback leading the team. You may abhor hunting Bambi, but if you have clients in Pennsylvania, you should know why no one answers the phone in November.

Here's a shortcut to keep up with pop culture and the daily happenings in the world: read *USA Today* with your morning coffee. It covers every subject from serious politics to light banter and does so in a basic manner. It is appropriate to refer to this newspaper as the *Cliff's Notes* of current events. Daily reading will make you familiar with most water-cooler topics and will keep you from looking like Dan Quayle caught in the headlights.

Be Able to Detect a Lie

It's a sad fact that people will lie to you. It's good to go into any relationship or conversation giving the other person the benefit of the doubt, but you have to be able to know when people are being dishonest. Now, you don't have to possess the skill of a CIA operative. You are going to get burned. Such is life. I'm talking about the ability to know when obvious lies are being tossed your way.

People display several mannerisms that tip off they are lying. I'm always on guard when people blink rapidly when they speak. In addition, liars look to change the subject prematurely. My favorite tipoff? Liars include too many unneeded details and have an answer for everything. (People telling the truth often say, "I don't know.") Study the various lie indicators and choose the ones that work for you.

Be Able to Make Small Talk at a Business Social Gathering

A huge factor in climbing the corporate ladder is being able to function well socially. Part of this involves being comfortable mingling with people you have just met in a social situation—in other words, being able to chatter at a social gathering. Here are some ideas:

- Remark on the surroundings. Look around and see if there is anything worth pointing out. Examples of location or occasion comments include: "This is a gorgeous room!" "Such incredible catering!" "I love this view!" Or, "Great dog!" Another useful opening is, "How do you know the host?"

- Ask open-ended questions. Closed questions, such as "Do you like to go to movies?" can be answered with a yes or no, and then you're stuck with coming up with another question. This situation gets tiring real fast. Instead, ask, "What kind of movies do you like?" or "What was the last good movie you saw?"

- Listen. When the other person is talking, poor conversationalists focus on trying to think of something to say next instead of hearing what is being said. Stop this. If you listen—really listen—to what is being said, you will have an interesting reply when the time comes to make one.

- Say the other person's name now and then. Not only does this help you to remember the name, but it's also a sign of respect.

- And here's a trick that works every time. When meeting a married couple, you are guaranteed a fascinating story by simply asking, "How did you two meet?" Just watch. Smiles will come to their face as they talk—for an hour.

Know Basic Science

No, you don't have to be able to explain Einstein's theory of relativity (in fact, I don't believe Einstein could explain it), but do have a casual understanding of the planetary system, the periodic table, and know that a light-year measures distance, not time. Be able to hold your own with a fifth grader.

Use Good Grammar

I'm not talking about using the word *whom* correctly. In fact, using that word correctly may leave you with the image of being a snobby –CS +BS. But do master some of the more common grammar complexities: it's/its, imply/infer, their/they're/there, and disreputable words or usages such as *irregardless* or *very unique*.[4]

Poor grammar lumps you in with a crowd of folks who share the traits of poor education and low common sense. This is not a group you want to be identified with.

Avoid Using "Punch" Words

This may seem minor on the surface and, indeed, occasional misuse of these terms won't label you a maroon, but regular use of the words that follow casts a glaring spotlight on your misuse of the language. Study these annoying adverbial abominations:

- *Actually.* This word is supposed to signify that something exists in reality, but it is often used just to add an extra punch to the sentence or as a substitute for saying, "Uhh . . . ."

- *Basically.* Use this word only to signify a simple or fundamental point.

---

[4]This is also critical in your writing. Remember this: each time someone tries to make a word plural by adding "'s," a puppy dies.

- *Honestly.* Repeated use of this word implies everything else you said was a lie.
- *Literally.* If you say, "He literally died laughing," there'd better be a corpse with a grin on its face.

Don't Agonize over Routine Decisions

There are some folks who make everything an issue. They will overanalyze the most routine situation. These are the same people who go to McDonald's every day, stare at the same menu board for seven minutes, and then order the same damn thing they have ordered every single day for the past 14 years.

I have a friend who has this habit. At first, it drove me nuts to see him analyze the most routine purchases. Even if he was buying a toaster or selecting a brand of canned soup, Allen would research every possible angle. *Consumer Reports* was his bible. After a while of exasperation with this (in my book) character flaw, I decided to let his quirk work to my advantage. Thanks to Allen, I now make decisions much more quickly. Here's how: whenever I need to buy something, I don't do any research; I just find out what Allen bought and then buy the same thing.

Handle Screw-ups with Grace

You will screw up. It happens. The trick is not to freak out when you stumble; your reaction will call attention to the slight error and hurt your perception far more than the original screw-up did. Here are some ideas for dealing graciously with embarrassing situations:

- Don't get flustered or show great distress. Most things seen as embarrassing are rarely even noticed by others, at least not in the magnitude you are feeling them. Overreacting to a small event is more harmful to your reputation than the event itself.

- Play the what-if game when you are going into a situation that may be awkward. Consider several possible scenarios and decide on your reaction before the event occurs.

- Never call attention to other people's embarrassing moments. You might be tempted to do this as a power play, but the effect will be the opposite. People will wonder, "What in the world was he *thinking?*"

- And when you make a mistake or screw up, don't make excuses or try to cover it up. Remember, Nixon didn't get in trouble because of Watergate, it was because of the cover-up. Bill Clinton wasn't impeached because of his shenanigans, it was for saying things like, "I didn't have sexual relations with that woman." And Martha Stewart didn't go to jail for insider trading; she went to jail because she lied to investigators.

You will occasionally do stupid things. Most of these acts will be overlooked as long as you don't shine a bright light on them.

Common sense   Never complain about your problems, because 80% of the people don't care and the other 20% are glad you have them.

Laugh at Yourself

When polled about what is the most attractive thing about a man, most women say a sense of humor. (This is not, of course, the number one item on men's list for women.) But remember this: A self-effacing sense of humor takes other issues off the table. If you poke fun at your receding hairline or even a silly mistake you just made, it takes the weapon out of your adversary's arsenal. It takes your image from being someone who just did something dumb to someone with healthy self-confidence.

Reject Stereotypes

Why is bigotry a sure sign of the lack of common sense? Because bigotry indicates a decision-making process based on an incredibly small sample. That's the intellectual explanation. The other explanation is that prejudices are the product of a small mind.

Here is a fact: your career will implode at the first indication of bigotry. Labeling people based on factors unrelated to them specifically is not just socially unacceptable, it's ignorant. And public displays of stupidity will brand you forever. Your image will not recover. I'm not declaring these things from a moral perspective—I'm talking about good business judgment and basic common sense.

Understand that I am not talking about political correctness, either. I abhor political correctness. I am talking about a simple judgment process. This perception of poor judgment can have a dramatically negative effect on your career. People will, for example, ask themselves things like, "Can we trust the decisions made on a $40 million account to someone who thinks all Muslims are anti-American?"

I know what is going through your mind right now. You are thinking, This is not 1958. People don't have prejudices anymore. Think again. Maybe they don't express them as blatantly, but they do exist! Besides, not all prejudices and stereotypes are so obvious. For instance, in America today, it is completely acceptable to poke fun at whites, people who are overweight, Christians, men, and Southerners. (Crap! I'm five for five.) But, this is not an intelligent thing to do. Although poking fun at people like me won't get you fired, it will get you labeled as someone void of common sense.

Argue Maturely

Argue civilly. Study how ten-year-old children disagree. Rather than having a respectful exchange of ideas, they roll their eyes and even laugh at their "opponent." Learn how to state your opinions firmly but respectfully, or you may end up looking like a ten-year-old (or a befuddled sitting vice president).

Know When to Quit

I'm not suggesting you be a quitter. In fact, persistence is a trait of successful people. I recall a TV show in which fledgling inventors appeared before a panel of entrepreneurs who were looking for inventions to invest in. One contestant demonstrated a table game he invented, sort of like Ping-Pong without paddles. The game was interesting, but it was apparent it would not be a big hit—it certainly did not have the type of potential that would motivate investors to fork over cash. The inventor began to weep when given the news that he would not receive funding. He then told the panel members he had tried to promote his game for ten years, had invested all his (substantial) savings, ended his career, and even suffered the breakup of his marriage because his wife simply got fed up. The panel's advice? Give up. He was destroying his life on a windmill that would never pan out. At some point, you need to heed the words of Mark Twain: *If at first you don't succeed, try, try again. And then give up. No sense in being a damn fool about it.*

So now I'll take my own advice. Because there is no way I can produce an all-inclusive list, it has to end somewhere. I think that will be here.

OK, Maybe One More Thing . . .

One last tip for avoiding the perception of lacking common sense: *Don't say dumb things.* This is easier said than done; all of us let some real silliness slip out from time to time. However, you can limit this exposure by taking a moment and running the sentence through your commonsense filter before blurting it out.

Perhaps this is a good time to poke fun at lawyers. (Actually, any time is a good time for this. It just fits in particularly well in this section.) Here are some questions asked in court by learned barristers; it's a pity they failed to run these questions through their mental filters before they spoke.

Q: Now doctor, isn't it true that when a person dies in his sleep, he doesn't know about it until the next morning?

Q: The youngest son, the twenty-year old, how old is he?

Q: Were you present when your picture was taken?

Q: Was it you or your younger brother who was killed in the war?

Q: You were there until the time you left, is that true?

Q: How many times have you committed suicide?

and

Q: So the date of conception of the baby was August 8th?

A: Yes.

Q: And what were you doing at that time?

and

Q: You say the stairs went down to the basement?

A: Yes.

Q: And these stairs, do they go up also?

and

Q: Doctor, how many autopsies have you performed on dead people?

A: All my autopsies are performed on dead people.

Summary

Common sense is often demonstrated best by *not* demonstrating a dearth of common sense. Sad fact: One dumb comment can wipe out a hundred brilliant ones. An absence of a negative statement carries as much weight as the presence of a positive one. Ergo, others will perceive you as having common sense simply because you have successfully avoided demonstrating a lack of it.

Heed this wisdom from +CS +BS guru Mark Twain: *It's better to be silent and thought a fool than to speak up and remove all doubt.*

Common Nonsense Based on Faulty Appeals

Appealing to Nonsense and Making It Personal

There are two ways to improve your overall performance in anything. The most obvious is to increase your output of brilliant things. I have found, however, that it is much easier—and effective—instead, to decrease the output of dumb stuff. Elimination of a negative is usually stronger than the addition of a positive. Perhaps my management philosophy also works with common sense. The most productive way to increase your common sense may be to eliminate any act that makes you appear to lack common sense.

People with good common sense speak and think logically. So, I guess it would be reasonable to say that people who do not use logic possess *common nonsense*. How can we identify common nonsense? Lines of (non)reasoning that tend to make the speaker appear foolish are referred to as *fallacies*. A fallacy is, put simply, an error in reasoning. (This differs from a factual error, which is simply being wrong about the facts.) To be more specific, a fallacy is an argument in which the premises given for the conclusion do not provide the needed degree of support—or, to put it another way, *common nonsense*.

In the next couple of chapters we're going to examine some of the more popular fallacies and see how they are often incorporated in our daily conversations and debates. You'll find you can build a great reputation for having good common sense simply by avoiding the use of these fallacies.

The first set of fallacies we explore is rather offensive oriented and often involves sharp words designed to put the listener on the defensive. These offensive weapons come in two forms—I call them *the Appeals* and *the Personals*. Let's first examine a myriad of common nonsense gems that tend to appeal to some factor unrelated to the issue being discussed.

Common Nonsense: Appeal to Authority

> His handsome, smiling face flashes on the TV screen. "I am not a doctor but I play one on television," he begins. "Hi, this is Tristan Temple from The Sexy and the Dying. After a hard day at the hospital, I often have a sore back. And when I feel that, I know I can get quick pain relief with Eat-Em-Up Aspirin. Trust me. It works.

Offering proof from an authority is a legitimate way to prove your point. So when does Appeal to Authority transition from being a strong rhetorical weapon to a babble of nonsense? This happens when the authority used simply does not have legitimate expertise in the subject being discussed.

Television commercials are an extreme example of this silliness, but there are many more subtle ways this is demonstrated. Watch the endorsements during a political campaign—are we really influenced by who Leonardo DiCaprio or Chuck Norris endorses for president?

This illegitimate reasoning can also occur when a true expert is cited. Unfortunately, these distinguished people are not experts in the fields they are commenting on. A senator gives his medical opinion about a woman in a coma. A former vice president makes bold declarations about climate change. An actor who played a medical examiner on a popular television show testifies before a congressional committee about the need for more funding to treat so-called "orphan diseases." A Hall-of-Fame baseball player explains that our immigration policy must be changed. Before you are convinced by the testimony of an authority, make sure that person's authority has something to do with the subject being discussed.

This fallacy also occurs when the authority being used is not identified. How often have you heard arguments beginning with, "I have a book that says . . . ," or perhaps, "All the top scientists agree . . . ," or, my personal favorite, "They say that . . ." Yes, it is a sad fact that in the world of common nonsense, "They" is the most powerful expert you can possibly cite.

Common Nonsense: Appeal to Common Practice

There was outrage during the 1970s directed at President Richard Nixon's abuses of his office. Although this furor eventually led to the collapse of his presidency, Nixon did have his defenders. His strongest supporters would cite Lyndon Johnson having the IRS audit his political enemies, and John Kennedy authorizing the wiretapping of Martin Luther King's private telephone calls. "Sure Nixon did some illegal things, but all of the presidents have skeletons in their closets. They all do it."

The fallacy of Appeal to Common Practice states that because most people do something, then it must be OK to do it. This fallacy is especially popular with teenagers who are trying to convince their parents to allow all sorts of outlandish behavior or extravagant purchases. Parents, how many times have you heard, "You have to let me [fill in the blank]. All of my friends are allowed to!" Where this fails the common sense test is that the mere fact that most people do something does not in any way justify the act.

Before we jump on yet another opportunity to mock our teenage philosophers, how many times have you heard someone in your company say, "Why do we do it that way? Because that's how everybody else does it."

Although it probably is true that most people cheat on their taxes, I do not recommend using that fact as a defense when you are hauled before a court on a felony tax charge.

Common sense   True, the early bird catches the worm, but don't forget that the early worm gets caught.

Common Nonsense: Appeal to Ignorance

> Theresa: *I believe that not only is there intelligent life on other planets, but that some of them have visited Earth.*
>
> Archie: *I can't accept that. Why do you believe such things?*
>
> Theresa: *Can you prove me wrong? No one has ever been able to prove that such beings do not exist!*

The Appeal to Ignorance assumes a statement must be true if it cannot—or has not yet—been proved false. As shallow as this line of reasoning seems to be, there are a myriad of examples of its use.

During the Red scare of the 1950s, populist Senator Joseph McCarthy became infamous for claiming to have a list of Communists who were working for the state department. When questioned about one of the names he had on the list, McCarthy remarked, "I do not have much information on this except the general statement of the agency that there is nothing in the files to disprove his Communist connections."

Many people took this absence of evidence as proof that the person was, indeed, a Communist. Senator McCarthy never produced any evidence against the people he labeled as committing treason. Yet despite this, McCarthy enjoyed great power and acclaim as he destroyed the lives of dozens of innocent Americans.

The Appeal to Ignorance can be a dangerous fallacy that places listeners on the defensive. It hopes to cause them to believe the statement is true merely because they cannot prove otherwise. Do not take the bait when faced with this common nonsense—just remind the fallacy-spouter that, in this country, the burden of proof resides with the person making the claim.

Common Nonsense: Appeal to Pity

> Gary was in a closed-door meeting with his boss. It seems that Gary had recently promoted a worker to supervisor and the new supervisor had already created turmoil in the plant. Gary's boss began: "I'm looking over the list of finalists you had to consider for the supervisor position. Cynthia has more seniority, Allen had the highest test scores, and Jose, by far, had the best performance reviews for three years in a row. What made you select Dexter for this job?"

Gary shifted uncomfortably in his seat. "True. All the other candidates sure look like better matches, but I had to give the job to Dexter. He's been having a pretty tough time lately. His wife has threatened to leave him and his sick kid—you know, the one with ichthagoocus— is costing a lot of money and he really needed the raise. Besides, Dexter's had his heart set on this promotion and I just couldn't let him down."

An Appeal to Pity occurs when reasonable facts are disregarded in favor of good old-fashioned pity. As nonsensical as this thinking may seem, such decisions are made regularly in our society. Kids (and adults!) are allowed a lot of slack because they "had a tough childhood." A player is given a roster spot only because "he's tried so hard." Celebrities are let off the hook because, well, they are celebrities and it would be a pity to see them hauled off to jail.

I ran across just such decision making several times in my operations career. I reviewed all proposed promotions to general manager with the supervisor wanting to make the promotion. Looking back, it was amazing how many of these proposed promotions—although ostensibly based on legitimate qualifications—had pity as the real basis. Usually the reasoning wasn't as blatant as the scene depicted earlier. Often, it was a tiebreaker between two candidates. Nonetheless, I must admit it was pity that got several folks their promotion.

I'm not trying to be coldhearted here. I'm really not. If you want to do something nice for someone who has had a rough time, well, go right ahead. Just be aware that you are doing it as an act of pity, not because a person's dysfunction is rational support for your actions.

Common Nonsense: Appeal to Flattery

Good afternoon, Mrs. Cleaver. And may I say you certainly look lovely today! By the way, I was wondering if I could . . . .

Here is how Appeal to Flattery works: instead of presenting evidence, the speaker just lays a great big ol' sloppy kiss on you. Appeal to Flattery is better known by more colorful terms, such as *apple polishing*. What they have in common is the desire to win your support by saying nice things to you rather than by delivering any rational facts.

Despite the transparency of such a ploy, Appeal to Flattery is remarkably effective. I can remember having an intense telephone conversation with a manager many years ago. He had been delivering substandard results in his region and I was on the brink of chewing him up real good. Just as I was getting my momentum going, he interrupted and successfully diverted my line of thinking. "Excuse me, Ken," he said, "but you sure do sound like you've lost some weight." I had to give him credit; I've never worked with anyone who could brown nose like him.

Common Nonsense: Appeal to Novelty

> Mike: So, what is this new management system the company is going to use? I think it's called Cute?
>
> Larry: Not Cute; it's KEWT. It's called the Keep 'Em Worried Today system. It's the newest way to run a corporation. There are all sorts of books hot off the press talking about it. It's the latest thing out of the think tanks.
>
> Mike: It seems to me that the way we have been doing things has worked just fine. I don't like the idea of changing everything around here without a good reason.
>
> Larry: Come on, Mike! You know we have to stay on the cutting edge. We've got to get KEWT or we're all going to be left behind counting dinosaurs!

Advertisers know the second most powerful message they can send is *It's New!* (What is number one? Yep, that would be *On Sale.*) Why is *new* such a powerful word?

Our culture tends to feel that new things are better than old. It seems progress implies that newer things are superior to older things. Even scientific theory backs up this concept—evolution proves the newest animals are the best, fittest, and most successful. Because of these factors, people often accept that a new thing or idea or concept must be better just because it is "the latest thing."

I spent a good chunk of my career with a fast-food company that shot to the top because of its edgy, contemporary culture. It took innovative risks and, for the longest time, these risks all paid off. The company had such a success rate, in fact, that its executives eventually believed their own bullshit thinking that any new idea must be a great one. After this culture was established, and new products and techniques were embraced almost automatically, the luck seemed to dry up quickly. After several new products and marketing campaigns bombed, the company backed off on its "it's great because it's new" culture.

This sort of reasoning is fallacious, of course. Just because something is new does not necessarily make it better. And if you think that Appeal to Novelty doesn't make a whole lot of common sense, then you're really going to love the next appeal.

Common Nonsense: Appeal to Tradition

Bill Brock, a Republican congressman from East Tennessee, was running for the U.S. Senate against a very popular Democratic incumbent. Campaigning one day in a rural area, he came upon a voter who declared that he would never vote for a Republican. When asked why, the farmer quickly replied, "My granddaddy was a Democrat and my Daddy was a Democrat, so I will always be a Democrat!"

Congressman Brock just had to bait him a bit. "Well, what if your granddaddy and your daddy had both been jackasses? What would that make you?"

"Well, I guess I would have been a Republican," was the quick response.

Appeal to Tradition assumes something is better just because things have always been done that way. Of course, just because something was done a certain way in the past does not, in and of itself, make it correct.

Tip   Suspect any argument or statement with the basis, "We've always done it this way."

This line of common nonsense is quite appealing to many folks. Lots of people like sticking with traditional methods and ideas. They are simply more comfortable with what they have been around longer. And, let's face it, it's a whole lot easier to stay with the old than to try out new things or ideas. Many people stay with tradition out of simple laziness. Another reason people stick with the past is because they may claim that the product or idea has "stood the test of time." Hey look, if you want to stick with a system because you believe it has proved itself, then that is, indeed, rational. But, if you are justifying something only because it has been done a certain way in the past, then that is just plain intellectually lazy.

There is another form of Appeal to Tradition that involves worshipping the past. Some people proclaim that something works because it was used by ancient civilizations. Grab one of those newspapers in the supermarket checkout line and read about miracle cures that produce amazing results.

Why? Because it was used by an ancient lost civilization! Let's apply some common sense here. Other than existing thousands of years ago, what qualifies a civilization that traded its daughters for goats to having created a miracle cure for cancer?

A recent folly predicted the world would end in 2012. How was this determined? For many people, it was an undeniable fact simply because someone found an ancient Mayan calendar that ended 2012. Those with no common sense claimed that because it was produced by an ancient civilization, it proved that the world would end in 2012. Those of us with common sense figure the reason the calendar expired in 2012 was because the writer probably just ran out of paper.

Common Nonsense: Appeal to Ridicule

> *My esteemed opponent believes that marriage licenses ought to be given to same-sex couples. This position is just plain ridiculous and the product of a silly intellect.*

When someone resorts to Appeal to Ridicule, he or she is replacing facts or evidence with mockery. This tactic is the rhetorical form of bullying. The logical error is obvious, but it is also quite effective and is often used by folks who lack the IQ of a comatose hamster. (See what I mean?)

This sort of reasoning is fallacious because mocking a claim does not show that it is false. However, regardless of the illegitimacy of this line of common nonsense, I must admit its use is often effective. When someone's opinion is ridiculed, it puts them on the defense. It often results in the mocked person backing down and the bully walking away with an immoral victory. Although the bully may win the argument battle, he has most certainly lost the common sense war.

Common Nonsense: Appeal to Spite

> *Darlene: Julianne has done an impressive job. I'm going to nominate her for Manager of the Year.*
>
> *Tina: Don't forget that she voted against you when you were up for the award last year.*
>
> *Darlene: Oh, that's right. She sure did. Well, there's no way I'm going to support her now.*

When people use Appeal to Spite reasoning, they substitute spite for evidence. This shows no common sense because an emotion does not count as a rational reason to be for or against a claim.

This all seems to be obvious nonsense when you study examples such as the one presented here, although the real test comes in everyday life. Pay close attention to conversations you overhear—or participate in—in the coming weeks. Notice how often conclusions are drawn using spite as the rationale. Now if your purpose is to get even, well go ahead and get your pound of flesh. Just call it what it is. You are acting to even the score; you're not using logic.

Tip   Many people act on the basis of spite. Knowing this, don't hand them a weapon to use against you. Take the high road.

The fallacies we just discussed attempt to influence you by appealing to some inner prejudice or need. There are some more examples of common nonsense that fall into this line of rhetoric. They tend to distract you from their lack of logic by touching a personal nerve. Perhaps the sting of the attack is just enough to cover up the spouting of the common nonsense.

Common Nonsense: Personal Attack

> *Michelle makes a speech in which she declares that a fetus is a human being, and therefore abortion is murder and is morally wrong. Todd reminds his wife that Michelle is just a goody-two-shoes Christian and can be ignored.*

A personal attack is committed when the person making a statement is attacked rather than attacking the statement itself. Common sense tells you that the argument and the person making it are two separate entities. Common sense also declares that no matter how revolting a person may be, that person is still capable of making true statements and of holding legitimate opinions.

'Nuff said.

Common sense   A person who is nice to you but rude to a waiter is not a nice person.

Common Nonsense: Spotlight

Jane and Kathy are preparing to board their flight to Washington. Jane pokes her travel partner and nods in the direction of another passenger who has arrived at the gate.

"Looks like we'd better change flights. This one's going to have a terrorist aboard!"

Why do you say that?" Kathy asks.

"Just look at him," replies Jane, "He's obviously a Muslim."

Kathy studies the man and sees that he is, indeed, dressed in a way that could identify him as Muslim. "OK, he's a Muslim. But why does that make him a terrorist?"

Jane looks at Kathy incredulously. "Are you serious? Ever seen a Muslim on television news that wasn't a radical? I'm telling you, if they are Muslim, they are either terrorists or they support terrorists. We're changing planes right now!"

The Spotlight fallacy is committed when it is assumed all members of a certain class or type are like those that receive the most news coverage. In other words, if one person is "in the spotlight," he immediately represents everyone he is similar to.

This line of reasoning, of course, defies all common sense. In fact, it could be inferred that the conclusion should be just the opposite. Because news stories generally feature exceptions to the everyday norm (otherwise, it wouldn't be news), it could be argued that most members of the targeted group are opposite from the individual in the spotlight!

People with good common sense do not believe that most people opposing abortions would like to murder abortion doctors. They don't assume everyone using the Internet is a child molester. They don't believe all Halloween candy is spiked with LSD. And they sure don't assume all members of a group are just like the one they saw on last light's 11 o'clock newscast.

Common Nonsense: Bandwagon

Comedian Jerry Seinfeld makes this observation about McDonald's famous billboards that use the Bandwagon approach to sell their product. "How insecure is this company? 'Eleven billion sold . . . .' All right! I'll have one."

Here is the first day's lesson from Advertising 101: *everybody is doing it; so should you.* In other words, everybody is buying our product, so you should buy it too. If an advertisement tells you, "It is no wonder a million people bought our product last year," they are leveraging the Bandwagon effect. So are ads promoting their product by saying, "We're number one!" (No doubt featuring a gorgeous lady waving an appropriate foam finger.)

Disturbing psychological fact: People often believe things merely because many other people believe the same things. Shrinks refer to this as a *herd instinct.* This common nonsense reasoning has been named after a practice in political campaigns during the early twentieth century in which candidates would ride a bandwagon through town and people would show their support by climbing aboard—thus the origin of the phrase *Climb aboard the bandwagon!*

Advertising is a rich source of bandwagon declarations. How often do we see a product justifying its purchase by claiming to be "the number one-selling pain reliever" or "the most popular choice for athletes?" Advertising executives know people can be easily influenced if led to believe that buying their product makes them one of the gang.

The use of this fallacy is certainly not limited to selling soap and soft drinks. Remember that political candidates originated the term itself. In 1952, General Dwight Eisenhower faced a small roadblock en route to the presidency. It seems he could offer very little political experience or expertise in government. He had a large constituency in the veterans who recognized his World War II skills, and he had a rather catchy campaign slogan. "I like Ike" was effective for motivating voters to jump aboard his bandwagon. Eisenhower rolled to a bandwagon victory, even though most voters couldn't identify his stance on any of the issues. Eisenhower's campaign managers knew, as many politicians have learned, that it is not the issues that motivate voters as much as feeling that they are voting like everybody else.

Just remember this the next time you are faced with a piece of Bandwagon common nonsense: *100,000 lemmings can't be wrong.*

Tip Avoid getting on someone else's bandwagon. You might be in the back when it goes off the cliff.

Common Nonsense: Guilt by Association

Randy: *I'm fed up with the IRS. I think we should get rid of the income tax and replace it with a national sales tax. That way there would be no loopholes and everyone would pay their fair share.*

Dan: *A national sales tax? That's the same thing spouted by Strom Redman.*

Randy: *Who's he?*

Dan: *Strom Redman is the Supreme Head Leader of the Communist Lover's Coalition and it's well known it wants to overthrow the government. You don't want to be supporting the Communists, do you? Are you a Commie, too?*

Guilt by Association argues that a position is wrong simply because it is also held by people or groups who are (rightfully or wrongly) not liked. What is wrong with this argument? Well, Adolph Hitler, John Dillinger, Lee Harvey Oswald, and every player on the 1996 New York Yankees all believed the world is round. Therefore, the world must be flat, right?

What gives this fallacy so much power is that no one wants to be associated with people they dislike. So if it is pointed out that a belief is also shared by a disreputable character, then many turn on that belief as quickly as they turn on the person they share it with. No one wants to be associated with Nazis, so people tend to shy away from any shared connections to that group. Of course, just because you don't want to be associated with some evil person does not mean that the shared belief is evil.

Guilt by Association is a great way to win an argument, albeit at the eventual cost of losing your reputation for having any common sense.

Common Nonsense: Generalizing

Bubba: *You know, Yankees sure do hate us Southerners.*

Skeeter: *Why do you say that?*

Bubba: *I was at an office party last night and met one of the big execs visiting from New Jersey. He said that he once hired two salesmen from Mississippi and they were the laziest workers he'd ever had. He said that, because of this, he would never hire any Southerners in his organization.*

Skeeter: *That doesn't sound like a good reason to "dis" everyone from the South. That kind of thinking really steams me.*

> *Bubba:* Yeah, I know what you mean. Do you think all Yankees are like him?

> *Skeeter:* Sure looks like it. Yessir, those Yankees sure do hate us Southerners.

Generalization is committed when a conclusion is made about a group based on an amazingly tiny sample. Note that a lot of prejudices get their origin from generalizations. Scotsmen are cheap, blacks can't swim, white men can't jump, Boomers have a low energy level, Christians are intolerant—the list is endless. But, trace back most prejudices and you will find a hastily made generalization at their root. For example, a sexist might conclude that all women are unfit to drive because his sister once crashed his Chevy.

Generalizations also often happen because of simple laziness. It is so much easier to leap to a conclusion than it is to do responsible research and gather legitimate samples.

I teach workshops to unemployed Boomers, helping them land the job for the next step in their careers. A major hurdle Boomers face are all the gross generalizations many employers have about this generation. Each Boomer seems to have to fight the group stereotypes that they are low energy, haven't kept up with new technology, won't respect a younger boss—the list is long. Because employers often throw a blanket of stereotypes over individuals based solely on generation generalizations, a lot of companies are passing up what could be dynamic star workers.

Your defense against generalizations is to ask for more proof or examples. If the person cannot come up with a legitimate population sample, then you can be sure he is just babbling some old-fashioned common nonsense.

Tip If someone uses a generalization argument against your position, ask for proof or examples.

Summary

That's a look at some of the prime examples of fallacies in which the speaker utters nonsense by making his or her comments rather personal. These rhetorical tactics often come with sharp daggers and the intent to ignore the argument, instead replacing it with rhetorical carnage. But, there is another approach for displaying common nonsense. These lines of (non)reasoning, intentional or not, display common nonsense in such a way that makes you want to ask, "You want to run that by me again?" We explore this phenomenon in the next chapter.

Common Nonsense Based on Muddled Logic

You Want To Run That One by Me Again?

The second group of Common nonsense statements features muddled logic. Often the product of lazy preparation or the simple disregard of fact collecting, these gems tend to offer scant support for their main argument. If you take a moment and dissect what was said, you'll decide that there's a complete lack of common sense being displayed.

Common Nonsense: The Non Sequitur

> *Life is life and fun is fun, but it's all so quiet when the goldfish die.*
>
> —Beryl Markham

Non sequitur is Latin for "it does not follow." Unlike most Latin phrases co-opted for rhetoric, this one is the perfect description of this common nonsense fallacy. A non sequitur is an argument that's conclusion does not follow its premises; there is a complete disconnect between the premise and its conclusion. If this fallacy was put into a mathematical formula, it would be 1 + 1 = potato.

For example: Many sober, educated people have seen objects in the sky that they have been unable to identify. Clearly, there is intelligent life on other planets. Or: My cousin lives in a large apartment building; his apartment must be really big. And here is one more: If we can put a man on the moon, then the Houston Astros should be able to win a World Series every once in a while.

Although many examples of the non sequitur border on the comedic (thus inspiring a popular comic strip by that name), there are a plethora of examples of the use of this illogic by usually commonsensical folks. In 2011, the Washington, DC, police began jailing people found with expired license tags on their cars. On his release from a night in jail, one "convict" commented to a police sergeant that his arrest seemed to be rather excessive for such a minor offense. The sergeant snapped—and I'm not making this up—"You wouldn't be saying that if someone you loved got hit by someone else with an expired registration."

Common Nonsense: Biased Statistics

The Greene County Teachers Association wanted to find out what citizens thought about raising local property taxes by 10% to build more classrooms. To save on postage, Henry only distributed the survey to teachers via the Association's monthly newsletter to its teachers. Henry was excited to report to the Association that the poll showed more than 95% of the public supported the tax increase.

Here is an interesting fact: 87.41% of all statistics are made up on the spot. And no wonder—quoting a statistic is a great way to prove your credibility in an argument. Quoting numbers (especially those that are carried out two decimal places) is a powerful debate weapon. But, as with any powerful weapon, great danger also lies here. Many statistics just aren't reliable, and they are a blockade to the exercise of good common sense.

The fallacy of Biased Statistics occurs whenever a person draws a conclusion based on a sample that is prejudiced. For example, if you want to know what most Americans think about eliminating all corporate income tax, a poll taken at a Tea Party rally would generate a biased statistic.

How do you avoid falling victim to this illogic? Whenever you are faced with a statistic, examine critically the field that was sampled. Is the population being polled a fair representation of the population in general?

Mark Twain once observed that there are three types of lies: lies, damned lies, and statistics. The use of these silly statistics is one reason why Twain made the observation.

Common Nonsense: Begging the Question

The minister was bringing his sermon to a passionate climax, comforting his flock on the power of God. "Yes, my friends, God most certainly does exist. How do I know? Because it says so in the Bible. And the Bible can be believed because it was, after all, given to us by God Himself!"

Begging the Question involves the use of circular logic. A conclusion is often proved because of itself. Many cases of question begging are blatant, whereas others can be quite subtle. Yogi Berra was a master of this fallacy. "No one ever goes to that restaurant anymore because it's always too crowded" is so blatant that it is a great gag line. A more subtle example of Begging the Question occurred during a San Francisco city council meeting, when members were discussing the elimination of drive-throughs at fast-food restaurants. One council member argued that no one wanted these features in restaurants because they were too busy and had long lines of cars.

Here's another example from pop culture. Frieda is amazed at all the news coverage given to Lindsay Lohan. "It makes no sense. She is just not newsworthy," she proclaims.

Her friend Marti replies, "Of course she is newsworthy. You see her picture everywhere. She is written about in all the magazines!" she reasons.

Your best defense against this type of common nonsense is just to pause for a moment and think about what was said. If the conclusion is used to prove the argument, then perhaps the argument can be discarded. After all, if it wasn't illegal then it wouldn't be against the law, would it?

Tip   To identify arguments that beg the question, simply ask yourself: Can the conclusion be used to prove the argument?

Common Nonsense: Black-and-White Thinking

During a heated debate in the U.S. Senate, a majority leader asked his colleagues, "Are you going to support this tenfold increase in foreign aid or do you prefer that Communists take over the world?"

Black-and-White Thinking occurs when you are presented with only two options, ignoring any other solutions or perspectives. This line of (non)reasoning can lead to an extremely intimidating argument, often leaving the victim speechless. Teenagers find this rhetoric quite effective: "Mom, either you buy me these designer jeans or else I'll be the most unpopular kid at school! You don't want everybody to hate me do you?"

This fallacy is used as an effective technique taught to all salespeople their first day on the job. "Do you want the red car or the blue one?" is a time-tested way to end the purchase discussion.

Your best defense to this common nonsense is to refuse to play this silly game. Reply, "Because there are a lot of other options I can pick from, I'm not going to make any of the choices you are suggesting."

Tip   Whenever someone asks you to pick one of two choices, pick neither. You have many other choices, including one to walk away from the person selling black-and-white solutions.

Common Nonsense: Split the Difference

Senator Boomer declares that the defense budget must be increased by $400 billion whereas Senator Flowers insists it should be cut by $250 billion. Because both senators are knowledgeable experts, it stands to reason that the proper thing to do is to increase the defense budget by $75 billion.

John declares that Superman can leap tall buildings in a single bound whereas Jess says that Superman doesn't even exist. Therefore, the proper opinion should be that Superman is powerful, but it probably takes him two or three bounds to leap a moderate-size building.

This pattern of fallacious logic occurs whenever one assumes that a position is correct simply because it lies between two extremes. Although finding middle ground can be an effective way to deal with some conflict, it is nonsense thinking to believe that a position is correct simply because it lies between two choices. The best defense against this illogic is to just say no. The numerical average of two positions is rarely the correct solution.

This discussion leads me to offering you a bit of management advice. (No extra charge for this; it's included in your initial purchase price.) There will be a day when two executives come to you with opposing solutions to a problem. You will have the urge to find a compromise—perhaps by splitting the difference between their proposals, with the hope of making them both happy with your Solomon–like decision. Avoid this. By compromising the decision, you create a third entity that has no sponsor, and no one will be accountable for its implementation. Instead of creating this orphan solution, pick one of the proposals and then hold the proponent responsible for its execution.

Common Nonsense: Gambler's Fallacy

A doctor is having his preoperative visit with a patient. "I have good news and bad news," he begins. "The bad news is that nine out of ten people I operate on die during the surgery." In response to the patient's look of horror, the doctor continues, "The good news is my last nine patients died. Looks like your surgery will be a success!"

The Gambler's Fallacy occurs when you assume that a departure from what occurs on average will be corrected in the short term. In other words, a person assumes a result is expected simply because what happened previously departs from what is expected during the long term. It is this type of illogic that results in all those luxurious buildings you see in Las Vegas.

Each time a coin is tossed, there is a 50% chance of it landing heads and a 50% chance of it landing tails. Suppose you toss a coin six times and it lands heads each time. The Gambler's Fallacy occurs if you assume the next flip of the coin produces tails, simply because it is due to come up. The fact is that each toss of the coin is independent of all others; the odds are 50/50 each time.

Although mathematical examples may seem obvious to us, we often make the error of the Gambler's Fallacy when we evaluate other things in our lives. Perhaps we choose to use a lawyer to litigate a case because she has lost her last five trials, so she must be due for success. Maybe we return to a steakhouse because the last four times you were there they cooked your steak wrong, and now they are finally due to grill it correctly.

You might remember that, in 1979, a large space station—Skylab—was scheduled to fall from orbit and come crashing to earth. Although scientists had calculated there was not even a small chance the debris would hit any person—the odds were calculated at more than ten billion to one—there was still a buzz for several weeks prior to the event as people pondered the possibility. One enterprising young man even made a bit of money selling hats constructed of tin foil with a purple propeller on top. His logic was that if the odds were ten billion to one against Skylab hitting any one individual, imagine what the odds were for it to smash into someone wearing an aluminum foil hat with a purple propeller.

Common sense   Never buy a Rolex watch from someone who is out of breath.

Common Nonsense: *Post Hoc, Ergo Propter Hoc*

There were 11 new liquor stores opened in our city in 2010. In 2011, church attendance increased by 8%. Obviously, opening more liquor stores will cause more people to go to church.

Post hoc, ergo propter hoc is Latin for "After this, therefore because of this." (I'm throwing a little Latin into this discussion because doing so makes me appear to be an intellectual.) This fallacy occurs whenever a person concludes that one event caused another simply because that event happened before the other event. For instance, Ralph lets out a huge burp and a massive thunderstorm begins. Although it is obviously absurd to blame the weather on Ralph, this type of misattribution is often presumed when dealing with routine problems. Consider these examples:

- Alfred buys gas from a new fuel station. A few miles down the road, he hears a funny sound coming from under the hood. Alfred concludes that the new gas station sold him some defective liquid dinosaurs.

- Terry's new computer has worked great for the past month, but then it crashes after he adds a new piece of software. The new program obviously wrecked his computer.

- Kim's daughter has a new boyfriend. Today her daughter announces that she is now a vegetarian. The new boyfriend must have convinced her to change her eating habits.

All these are example for the *Post Hoc, Ergo Propter Hoc* fallacy. You just can't assume that something that happened before caused something else to happen. And please note that the opposite isn't true either. The new gasoline may very well be the cause of the knocking engine, the new software certainly may contain a virus, and the new boyfriend might have influenced Kim's daughter to eat nuts instead of meat. Indeed, all these things may be causes, but you can't draw this conclusion just because they happened before the event. You need more facts.

Here's another example of *Post Hoc* in action, courtesy of the 2011 debates for the Republican presidential nomination. Mitt Romney stated, "Now we have more chronic long-term unemployment than this country has ever seen before, we've got housing prices continuing to decline, and we have foreclosures at record levels. This president has failed." By making this declaration, Romney is saying that the president's previous actions are responsible for all these bad things that happened. His argument was that because Barack Obama was elected president, the economy tanked, therefore President Obama is responsible for all that has happened to the economy. (You will note that Democrats used this same logic in evaluating the economy, declaring that because George W. Bush was in office before the economic collapse, it all must be Bush's fault.) Although the conclusion might be valid, the timing is not enough by itself to prove the conclusion. More evidence is needed to tie Obama's actions to the factors that Romney cited.

Post Hoc fallacies are typically committed because people are simply not careful enough when they reason. It is easier to jump to a conclusion than to investigate the root of the problem. And this is your defense when faced with *Post Hoc* illogic. Ask for more facts. Investigate. Seek more evidence.

You will note that many superstitions are based on *Post Hoc* reasoning. For example, a famous quarterback once failed to shave before a game and then had a particularly successful day on the field. For the rest of his career, the quarterback refused to shave on game day.

Tip   When faced with a *Post Hoc* illogical argument, ask for more facts. More facts eventually lead to the truth.

Common Nonsense: Red Herring

Prosecutor: ... and for all those reasons, you should find Oliver J. Shannahan guilty of the cold-blooded murder of Nichole Shannahan.

Defense attorney: But the real issue is that this city's police department is packed with racists. Every single member hates Irishmen.

The name of this fallacy comes from the sport of fox hunting. To train the dogs, a smoked herring, which is red, is dragged across the trail of the fox, threatening to throw the hounds off the scent. Thus, a *red herring* is an argument in which an irrelevant topic is presented to divert attention from the original issue.

The Red Herring device is often used in debating political issues, particularly those that tend to be emotionally charged. Some Red Herring arguments can get downright visceral, such as this bumper sticker seen in the 1980s:

More people died in the back seat of Ted Kennedy's car than at Three Mile Island.

And then there is this red herring, from former president Jimmy Carter:

I think an overwhelming portion of the intensely demonstrated animosity toward President Barack Obama is based on the fact that he is a black man.

A loud and hostile voice is often used by those making a Red Herring argument. The goal is to enflame the debate, diverting all attention from the real issue at hand. Often, the Red Herring is used to get audience members to debate the new issue among themselves, losing sight of the original issue.

When dealing with someone using a Red Herring argument, step back and take a deep breath, then point out that he or she is completely off the subject and is not showing a whole lot of common sense.

Common Nonsense: Straw Man

> Tamara: I think we need to provide a good education for all children, even those that might be illegal aliens.
>
> Tom: For real? Why would you want to give the illegals free housing, food stamps, and big welfare checks? All that does is encourage more lawbreakers to invade our country!

Imagine a fight in which one of the combatants builds a man out of straw, attacks it, then proclaims victory while the real opponent stands by untouched. This is the nature of a Straw Man argument. The Straw Man fallacy occurs when a person's actual position is ignored and an outrageous or exaggerated version is substituted. This new position, because it is so extreme, is easy to argue against. This sort of "reasoning" is fallacious because attacking a distorted version of a position simply does not constitute an attack on the position itself.

The Straw Man argument is one of the most often-used rhetorical devices in political debates. Pay close attention when candidates debate on TV (really, just joint press conferences). Notice how they ignore their opponent's actual position and attack a somewhat-related version.

Common sense   Nothing is fool proof. Fools are ingenious.

Common Nonsense: Two Wrongs Make a Right

> Joseph makes his daily purchase at a convenience store. He hands the clerk a $10 bill to cover the cost of the extralarge root beer. When Joseph gets back to his car, he discovers that the clerk has given him change for $20. Joseph considers returning the money, but because he has been shortchanged several times at various stores, he decides it is his right to keep the extra money.

Two Wrongs Make a Right is a fallacy in which an action is justified by claiming the person would do—or has done—the same thing to him. OK. The fact is, this line of thinking really should be resolved after the first few months of kindergarten. We all accept the notion that the Two Wrongs theory is morally wrong, but many people still subscribe to the principal on a logic basis.

We see this line of thinking used by terrorists, who justify the killing of innocents by stating that their opposition has done the same thing to their people. Many will defend an athlete lying to Congress about steroid use because some members of Congress often lie to their constituents. And many good folks justify otherwise unconscionable actions with the simple phrase, "Everybody does it."

In his book *It Didn't Start With Watergate*, Victor Lasky points out that a legal precedent is created if a set of immoral things are done and left unprosecuted. People who do the same wrongs in the future should, rationally, expect to get away with them as well. As an example, Lasky points to John Kennedy's wire-tapping of Martin Luther King, Jr., and Richard Nixon's crisis with Watergate. I can well remember the many arguments propounded during this time, defending President Nixon, including, "They all do it." Indeed, they did, but it's a pretty weak defense for a criminal act.

The best response to this argument I have seen is: Two wrongs don't make a right, but three lefts do.

Common Nonsense: Slippery Slope

Andy: Well, Barney, you know we always give the truck drivers an extra five miles an hour so they can make it up Turner's Grade.

Barney: Now Andy, if you let them take 30, they'll take 35. If you let them take 35, they'll take 40. If you let them take 40, they'll take 45. I say we gotta nip it! Nip it in the bud!

This commonsense blockade is also known as the Camel's Nose because of this legend:

One cold night, as an Arab traveler sat in his tent, his camel poked his nose under the flap and said, "It sure is cold out here. May I put my nose in your tent?"

The traveler agreed to this small accommodation, then rolled over and went to sleep. Later, the man awoke to find that the camel had now put his head and neck inside as well.

"You know," the camel remarked, "I'll only take up a little more room if you'll let me place my front legs inside the tent."

The man agreed and moved over a bit to make room in the small tent.

Finally, the camel said, "How about letting me stand wholly inside. It's just so darn cold out here."

The man sighed and replied, "Yeah, OK. You've come this far, you might as well come on in." So the camel crowded into the tent. The man soon fell asleep, but when he awoke the next morning, he found himself outside in the cold and the camel had the tent all to himself.

The Slippery Slope is a fallacy in which it is asserted that you can't agree to one event simply because doing so would cause an inevitable cascade of progressively worse events to happen. This sort of "reasoning" is fallacious because, unless further proof is presented, there is no reason to believe that one event must inevitably follow from another. This (il)logic is especially clear in cases when there is a significant number of steps between one event and another.

The Slippery Slope argument is often heard in debates about temporary tax increases: "If we open that door, they'll just raise more taxes next year." Or remember when the Nazis wanted to march in Skokie, Illinois (which has a large Jewish population)? Many wanted to ban the march, but it was argued that if it was stopped, it would lead to all unpopular marches being forbidden and eventually to the elimination of all First Amendment rights. And, history records that the Slippery Slope argument was used to justify our involvement in Vietnam. "If we let the Communists take over Vietnam, they'll take all of Southeast Asia. And then all of Asia. And pretty soon, they'll be parading their tanks and missiles right down Pennsylvania Avenue."

On the day of the tenth anniversary of 9/11, the New York Mets wanted to wear hats honoring the police and fire heroes of that day. Major League Baseball forbids this tribute, because the league previously ruled all uniforms could only include sports logos. Former Mets player Todd Zeille observed, "I find it ironic that ten years later they still can't get [the rule changed] for one day of tribute. I guess they feel it's a slippery slope or something."

Slippery slopes are slippery in more ways than one. Aside from sliding from one argument to another, there can also be sliding from one level of discussion to another. There is nothing wrong with using this type of argument in a rational discussion, if it can be demonstrated that the progression of events truly is inevitable. For instance, you could reasonably argue that lowering the legal age for purchasing cigarettes will cause youth to begin smoking earlier, which will lead to increased lung cancer rates, which will lead to premature deaths for thousands of people. This argument does make sense. However, beware of statements that indicate the inevitability of a future disaster rising from one early incident; this (non) reasoning doesn't demonstrate credible common sense at all.

■ **Tip** Be especially wary of slippery slope arguments. Most are designed to draw out your fears. They also act as smokescreens by taking your attention off one problem while highlighting a completely different one. Refuting these types of arguments is simple: just ask for the proof that suggests one event will lead to a whole barrelful of unwanted results.

Common Nonsense: Tail Wagging the Dog

A governor is holding a press conference to announce a bold, new initiative to fight poverty in her state. She declares, "The poverty rate is at an all-time high. We cannot have this and we must take meaningful, decisive action. Therefore, I am issuing this executive order that will immediately reduce the poverty rate by almost 10%!" When the press reviews the new executive order, it discovers that the definition of poverty has been changed. Now, a family only qualifies as impoverished if its annual income is less than $9,000 instead of less than $10,000, as the definition maintained previously.

Tail Wagging the Dog means to cause a desired result by redefining the issue or by changing the way it is measured. For instance, we all know that a dog wags its tail when it is happy. So, to have a happy dog, a person subscribing to this philosophy simply reaches down and wags the dog's tail for him. Wagging tail, ergo happy dog.

Now these examples are obviously silly, but such rationale is often used in business and politics. Our educational system showcases a prime example of Tail Wagging the Dog. Schools use SAT test results to measure schools' effectiveness in teaching. Higher scores indicate that the schools are doing a better job in teaching. So, to get higher scores on the SAT, many schools offer programs that teach students test-taking skills. Students have been able to record much higher scores by knowing the ways to interpret the questions and answers. Because higher scores are produced, schools must be doing a better job of teaching their students.

True story: Because the scores on police recruiting tests had dropped dramatically for the past three years, city officials were worried that the quality of their new police officers was regressing. In an effort to upgrade the quality of its police force, the city made the test much easier. Local officials were pleased when the test results showed strong improvement.

They were excited that they were now well on their way to building a great public safety agency.

Pay close attention when someone seems to be solving a complex problem a bit too easily. Chances are strong that there is some tail wagging going on—and that simply defies all common sense.

Note Politicians often engage in activities or make decisions that cause the tail to wag the dog. They'll point to the wagging tail as proof that whatever they are saying or recommending makes a lot of sense and is good for both me and you. Beware.

Summary

To maintain the best possible image of possessing good common sense, it is critical you avoid the use of rhetorical gimmicks. Take the time to construct your arguments with solid facts. Think through your case before presenting it. Ask yourself: Does this make sense?

And recognize the following when evaluating statements made by others: although commonsense blockades may be intentional, they are generally just the product of some spur-of-the-moment muddled thinking. The best way to deal with these rhetorical hiccups is to step back, take a deep breath, and say, "Huh? You want to run that one by me again?"

Urban Legends, Conspiracies, and Other Perversions of the Truth

The Absence of Common Sense

Technology now allows us to have the entire world's knowledge literally in the palm of our hands. We can communicate anywhere in the world in an instant. We can attend great universities, concerts, churches, or symposiums without leaving our sofa. So what do we use this amazing resource for? Primarily broadcasting funny stories, tweeting about Lindsay Lohan's latest exploits, and e-mailing pictures of our cat.

Perhaps I exaggerate, but only by a little bit. Our ability to communicate quickly has allowed us to dispense as much nonsense as knowledge. And, because things in writing seem to be more believable than simple word of mouth,[1] this nonsense has taken on a sense of believability unlike similar stories of the past.

Let's look at some of these perverted uses of our First Amendment rights and examine the common nonsense dispersed via urban legends, conspiracy theories, and other scandalous sad, silly stories.

Urban Legends

We've all heard them. Usually, they happened to a friend of a friend's second cousin, and in almost every case they're completely untrue. Still, some urban legends—stories that seem like they could be true and therefore probably are (maybe)—have managed to gain a remarkable amount of credibility. From creepy folklore to rumors about celebrities and politicians, urban legends quickly gain a popular following.

Many urban legends depict horrific crimes, contaminated foods, or other situations that would affect many people. Anyone believing such stories might feel compelled to warn loved ones. Frequently, news organizations, school officials and even police departments have issued warnings concerning the latest threat. For instance, in one mass-distributed urban legend, street gang members would drive without headlights until a motorist responded with the traditional flashing of headlights (to indicate to drivers that their headlights were not on), whereupon a new gang member was required to murder the citizen as an initiation rite. In addition to this urban legend being passed by word of mouth at parties and family gatherings, one police department—Nassau County, Florida—distributed their copy of the rumor to all city departments and the general public. Even the Minister of Defence for Canada forwarded an urgent security warning concerning this presumed danger to all Ontario Members of Parliament.

Let's look at some of the more popular urban legends we have been blessed with. We'll also take the opportunity to consider why the application of a little common sense would have brought the stories to a quick close.

---

[1] "Hey! If it's on the Internet, it has to be true!"

The Manufactured Chicken

Here is one of the more famous uses of Internet nonsense. This libelous rumor has been circulating for about ten years.

Subject: Boycott KFC

KFC has been a part of our American traditions for many years. Many people eat at KFC every day. Do they really know what they are eating?

During a recent study of KFC done at the University of New Hampshire, they found some very upsetting facts. First of all, have you noticed that just recently the company has changed their name? Kentucky Fried Chicken has become KFC. Do you know why? We thought the real reason was because of the "FRIED" food issue. It's not. The reason why they call it KFC is because they cannot use the word chicken anymore. Why? KFC does not use real chickens!

These so-called "chickens" are kept alive by tubes inserted into their bodies to pump in nutrients. They have no beaks, no feathers, and no feet. This is great for KFC because they do not have to pay so much for their production costs. There is no more plucking of the feathers or the removal of the beaks and feet.

The government has told them to change all of their menus so they do not say chicken anywhere. If you look closely, you will notice this. Listen to their commercials, I guarantee you will not see or hear the word chicken.

Please forward this message to as many people as you can. Together we can make KFC start using real chicken again.

I'm no geneticist, but I will bet you a dollar that the very idea of mass-producing genetically altered, intravenously fed chickens without feathers, beaks, or feet is science fiction. We are asked to believe that a company could save money by doing this. But according to KFC's own statistics, it sells more than 575 million birds a year! By what stretch of the imagination could it be cheaper to grow that many "organisms" in some vast, high-tech laboratory?

Although the company dumped its Kentucky Fried Chicken brand name more than a decade ago to emphasize product variety, it still uses the "forbidden" word in its advertising and in-store signage. Remember the TV jingle, "We Do Chicken Right!"? That was KFC. When asked if there's any truth whatsoever to the allegations, Michael Tierney, KFC's Director of

Public Affairs, answered, "Of course not. Any thinking adult would know it's absolutely absurd."

■ **Common sense**   Just because you have the right to do something doesn't mean it's the right thing to do.

McWorms

The rumor of a company secretly using genetically altered chickens is closely associated with a rumor that ran rampant during the 1970s. I was, at the time, running a small hamburger chain in Tennessee. The scandal making the rounds was the "fact" that all the hamburger chains were grinding worms in with their hamburger to reduce costs.

McDonald's was hit hardest with this, although all chains, including Wendy's, Krystal, and little chains such as mine, saw their sales fall and were subject to a plethora of customers making irate phone calls. The public relations departments of these chains were faced with a dilemma. Should they address this ridiculous rumor or ignore it and let it play out? If they addressed it, they may be able to refute the rumor; at the same time, however, they would be telling millions of people about the claim who had never heard the rumor. By dispelling the rumor, they could be actually fueling it!

The course chosen was for everyone to advertise/brag about the quality of their beef, adding the tagline "We use only 100% premium beef." Worms, of course, were never mentioned. It didn't take long for this rumor to fizzle; perhaps folks just found another one to follow. It's a shame that so much money had to be used to address such idiocy when a little dose of common sense would have stopped it in its tracks. How's that? Here's the deciding fact: Worms cost about $45.00 per pound; the highest premium ground beef is just $3.75 a pound.

Satanic Profits

Here is an urban legend that has been floating out there since the 1970s. The legend analyzes the logo for Procter & Gamble and has somehow interpreted it as a satanic symbol. According to the legend, Procter & Gamble is owned and operated by Satan worshippers and the profits are donated to the Church of Satan.

Without examining the facts, many people signed petitions against Procter & Gamble and boycotted their products. The company tried every strategy it could muster, even engaging the services of Billy Graham. Procter & Gamble eventually won $19.25 million in a civil lawsuit filed against four former Amway distributors accused of spreading the false rumors. Unfortunately, Procter & Gamble learned that the harder they worked to prove the rumor was false, the more people actually started to believe it. ("It must be true if the company is fighting it so hard," was their line of "reasoning.")

This devastating urban legend only began to go away when the company terminated the use of their logo. And although Procter & Gamble has not used the logo for years, the legend still pops up from time to time among people without a shred on common sense.

Reverse Automatic Teller Machine Code

See this important message below.

Subject: Reverse Pin Numbers Can Thwart Robbers

I just found out that should you ever be forced to withdraw monies from an ATM machine, you can notify the police by entering your PIN in reverse. The machine will still give you the money you requested, but, unknown to the robber, the police will be dispatched immediately to help you. The broadcast stated that this method of calling the police is very seldom used because people don't know it exists, and it might mean the difference between life and death. Hopefully, none of you will have to use this, but I wanted to pass it along just in case you haven't heard of it. Please pass it along to everyone possible.

According to a story published in the St. Louis *Post-Dispatch* last year, bankers are opposed to the reverse personal identification number (PIN) system because of safety concerns. They worry that ATM users might hesitate or fumble while trying to enter their PIN backward under duress, possibly increasing the chances of violence. But perhaps more significant: What about those PINs that are palindromes? How do you call the cops if your PIN is 1991?

Common sense "I bring out the worst in my enemies, and that's how I get them to defeat themselves."—*Roy Cohn*

The Key Ring

Subject: SECURITY ALERT—Nigerians at Gas Station

Syndicates made up of Nigerians are giving free keyrings at gas stations. Don't accept them because the key rings have a tracking device that allows them to follow you.

Forward this alert to friends and family. A friend alerted me on the above and indicated that these guys just select their seemingly well-to-do potential victims and play the trick.

The key holders, I am told, are too beautiful to resist collecting, but remember, you may end up paying more, including your life, if you can't resist.

The application of just a bit of common sense would kill this urban legend, but let's just examine one line of thought. Why would they need to follow you? All this would do is take them to a place where a nice car is parked. The same thing can be accomplished much more easily and cheaply by simply driving around a neighborhood until they spot a car they'd like to steal.

Sniper Fred

This one made the rounds in 2004 upon the death of TV's Mr. Rogers.

On another note, there was this wimpy little man (who just passed away) on PBS, gentle and quiet. Mr. Rogers is another of those you would least suspect of being anything but what he now portrays to our youth. But Mr. Rogers was a U.S. Navy Seal, combat-proven in Vietnam with more than 25 confirmed kills to his name. He wore a long-sleeve sweater to cover the many tattoos on his forearm and biceps. He was a master in small arms and hand-to-hand combat, able to disarm or kill in a heartbeat. He hid that away and won our hearts with his quiet wit and charm.

Yes, Fred Rogers did win our hearts, but the rest of the story is absolute baloney. After graduating with a degree in music in 1951, he immediately embarked on a broadcasting career. This career continued for nearly 50 years, even while he studied for a Bachelor of Divinity degree and became an ordained minister in 1962. Far from hiding a secret past as a trained killer, Fred Rogers was a truly gentle soul who devoted his entire adult life to educating and bettering the lives of children. And that is how he deserves to be remembered.

▨ **Common sense**   It doesn't take a brave dog to bark at the bones of a lion.

Halloween Terrors

Halloween mayhem is by far the most popular urban legend, and the most widely believed to be true. It has almost become a fact in some folks' minds that unscrupulous people are handing out poisoned candy to unsuspicious children on Halloween. This has become a staple of urban legend lore, in part as a result of the horrifying nature of the act and because of the mass media coverage that false claims of poisoned Halloween treats have received. Hospitals routinely open their doors to x-ray candy for fear that the Milky Way bar has needles hidden in it. Even Jesse Jackson once called for the elimination of the holiday by declaring, "Every year, we read tragic stories of children who are bloodied by sick tricks. They bite on an apple and are cut with a hidden razor blade." Parents forbid their kids from enjoying this children's festival because they feel the neighborhood is full of evil predators eager to harm their children.

Here is the fact: There is just one documented case of tampered candy being knowingly distributed to a child. This rumor began in Houston when a father gave a cyanide-laced Pixy Stix to his own child with the intention of killing him and collecting the insurance money. That is the only case of doctored or altered candy being given out at Halloween, and it had nothing to do with neighborhood trick-or-treating.

Such a rumor can be easily debunked by simply analyzing the crime. For each child, trick-or-treating takes place in a relatively small area. If someone was passing out altered or poisoned candy, he or she could be easily identified and arrested. If such a crime was happening on a mass scale—as the legend implies—our prisons would be filled with these perpetrators. The fact is, not one person is serving time for such a crime, because no one has committed such an evil act.

The Kidney Heist

The most persistent urban legend, The Kidney Heist, has been immortalized on the Internet, in television shows, and even in a few movies. In most versions, a business traveler is relaxing in a bar when a stranger strikes up a conversation and then offers to buy him a drink. After taking a few sips, the traveler becomes woozy and then blacks out, only to awaken in a hotel room bathtub covered with ice. There is a phone next to him and a note that says to call 911 immediately. When the paramedics arrive, the person learns that one of his kidneys has been harvested by people who hope to sell it on the black market.

This message sparked an avalanche of phone calls to local authorities, even prompting the New Orleans Police Department to publish an official statement to calm public fears.

It's a scenario that has taken many forms. I first heard it myself many years ago from a friend who'd heard it from another friend, whose mother swore it had happened to a distant cousin. Before New Orleans, people said it happened in Houston; before Houston, Las Vegas—where an unsuspecting tourist was drugged in his hotel room by a prostitute and woke up the next morning, supposedly, in a bathtub full of ice, minus a kidney.

"There is absolutely no evidence of such activity ever occurring in the U.S. or any other industrialized country," says the United Network for Organ Sharing. "While the tale sounds credible enough to some listeners, it has no basis in the reality of organ transplantation."

To dispel this legend quickly, you need to understand a bit about organ transplantation. It's not possible for a kidney transplant—or any organ transplant—to take place outside properly equipped medical facilities. The removal, transport, and transplantation of kidneys involve a sterile setting, precise timing, and the support of so many highly trained personnel that kidney removal for transplantation simply cannot be accomplished in a hotel room. The National Kidney Foundation has repeatedly issued requests for any victim of such a crime to come forward. None have.

Unfortunately, this legend has put lives at risk. In the 1990s, rumors spread in Guatemala that Americans were kidnapping local children and harvesting their organs for transplantation in the United States. Several U.S. citizens and Europeans were attacked by mobs who believed the rumors to be true. An American woman was severely beaten and remains critically impaired.

Organizations that facilitate organ transplants are concerned this legend may be partly responsible for a reduction in the number of volunteer donors, resulting in needless deaths among seriously ill patients awaiting transplants.

Wow. This really brings it home. As a man waiting his turn on the kidney transplant list—for about five years now—I hate to think my survival hopes may be dashed by a silly little (harmless) urban legend.[2]

Urban legends have been with us since Adam, but their spread was somewhat stifled by slow communication—word of mouth and the U.S. Postal Service. All that has changed during the past 20 years with the explosion of the Internet. Let's look at how the Internet adds fuel to raging fires.

The Internet

In the not-so-distant past, every corner pub seemed to feature a drunk guy at the end of the bar spouting his unique perspective on all the world's problems to people trying to escape from all the world's problems. Today, you don't have to visit a pub to have the world explained, all you have to do is power up your computer and access the Internet. It's as if millions of inebriated scholars leaped from the end of the bar and landed in your lap.

Nonsense from the Right

The latest idiocy from my friends on the Right is to proclaim, "Obama is going to change the law so he can get elected to a third term." Besides the handwringing on Facebook posts, ads are appearing on conservative web sites begging for donations to stop this power grab.

Let's dissect this interesting claim and perhaps help some of my trembling friends to relax. First of all, a president cannot change a law; that takes an act of Congress. However, this restriction of not holding the presidential office for more than two terms is not in the form of a law; it is in the Constitution. So for Obama to serve again, the Constitution would have to be changed. This is not an easy thing to do. It is so hard, in fact, that in its 275-year, it has only been changed 28 times. All the actions listed below must occur for this to happen.

---

[2] If you enjoy this book, you might want to say "thank you" by letting me have one of your kidneys. If not me, think about donating to someone in your community. There is no greater gift than the gift of life. For further information, contact the National Kidney Foundation at kidney.org.

- Step 1: Two thirds of the Senate must approve. The Senate has 100 members, so 67 would have to vote to approve. As of 2013, 55 Senators are Democrats, 45 Republican. So to get approval in the Senate, every Democrat (many with presidential ambitions of their own) would have to vote yes, along with 12 of the Republicans. How likely is this?

- Step 2: An even tougher barrier exists in the House of Representatives. As of 2013, 232 of its 435 members are Republicans and most (124) of them would have to join *all* 203 Democrats to pass the proposed amendment. How likely is this?

- Step 3: After the proposed amendment passes both houses of Congress by a two-thirds margin, it then must be submitted to the states for ratification. To be ratified, threefourths of the states must approve. So, with 50 states, 38 of them must support the new amendment. Obama won 26 states in the 2012 election; Romney won 24. So to be ratified, the amendment must pass in all the states that supported Obama, in addition to half the states that voted for Romney. How likely is this?

It is more likely that George W. Bush and Mitt Romney run off to California and marry each other than for *all* these things to happen. The notion that Obama will somehow be able to run for a third term defies all common sense, and the right-wingers out there could better spend their time worrying about our leaders having their minds taken over by invaders from the planet Vulcan. Which is far more likely than an Obama third term.

This is *one* example of the nonsense that floods in from the Right side of the political spectrum. But, the Right certainly does not have a monopoly on silly logic. Let's look at an example of a commonsense assault from the left.

Common sense   Never judge a book by its movie.

Nonsense from the Left

One of the forms common nonsense takes is hypocrisy. Here is a blatant example of this, courtesy of many of my friends on the Left.

During the junior Bush years, there was rarely a day that newscasts didn't sport an antiwar march denouncing President George W. Bush and the war in Iraq. Posters showing blood dripping from Bush's fangs and chants of "Bush lied and people died" were the features of these mass gatherings.

I never questioned the sincerity of these protesters. Although a rather loyal Bush supporter, I recognized the passion associated with a war and the deaths of our next generation. These folks were certainly caring, concerned citizens who wanted to see this nightmare stopped.

In October 2007, Obama proclaimed, "I will promise you this: that if we have not gotten our troops out by the time I am president, it is the first thing I will do. I will get our troops home. We will bring an end to this war. You can take that to the bank." Speaking of Iraq in February 2008, candidate Barack Obama said, "I opposed this war in 2002. I will bring this war to an end in 2009. It is time to bring our troops home." The following month, under fire from Hillary Clinton, he reiterated, "I was opposed to this war in 2002. . . . I have been against it in 2002, 2003, 2004, 5, 6, 7, 8 and I will bring this war to an end in 2009."

Few would argue that it was this opposition to the war that heavily contributed to Barack Obama's overwhelming election in 2008. This passionate antiwar movement contributed heavily and enthusiastically to his election. And there was great glee when he took office in 2009, looking forward to his ending the war as well as closing the military prison at Guantanamo.

But an odd thing occurred. Guantanamo was not closed in a year. In fact, five years later, there is no talk of it ever closing. And more important, our troops were not brought home. In fact, most of Bush's war policies were actually expanded for a while. The new president tripled President Bush's troop levels in Afghanistan. Although the president eventually declared "the official end to Operation Iraqi Freedom and combat operations by United States forces in Iraq," we still have 50,000 troops there, hardly what Senator Obama promised.

I have written off this reversal to President Obama learning some things when he took office that he didn't know when he was a candidate. He had a different understanding and made the proper decisions in response to them. When I speak of hypocrisy on the Left, I'm not referring to the actions of President Obama. I am speaking of the actions—or lack thereof—of the antiwar protesters.

All the thousands of passionate war protesters stopped their opposition the day George W. Bush retired. No more marches, no pictures of Obama with fangs—really, no public discourse.

How could such passion and concern dry up overnight? Why did the protest come to an abrupt halt on January 20, 2009? You have to conclude that these protesters were not opposed to war; they merely opposed George W. Bush. Hypocrisy is an ugly manifestation of common nonsense.

Nonsense as News

Shortly after 9/11 a photo began to circulate showing a tourist standing atop one of the World Trade Centers with an airplane in the background about to strike the tower. The accompanying story explained how the tourist's camera was found in the wreckage but the tourist remained missing. Here are two reasons proving the picture was fake:

- The tower containing the observation deck was the second one struck. Do you really think the fellow would hang around after seeing the first tower destroyed?

- The observation deck was not even open at the time the tower was struck.

Aside from all the very inconsistent details in the picture the story already seemed completely improbable this photo still pops up from time to time on the Internet.

Tip   To debunk news stories too preposterous to be true, use some common sense and look for facts. This is usually enough to highlight news nonsense.

Nonsense in Folklore

The similarities in the lives of Abraham Lincoln and John F. Kennedy have become so ingrained that it is often taught in high school history classes. Note:

- Both were elected to the House of Representatives in '46.

- Both were elected to the presidency in '60.

- Both their predecessors left office in their 70s and retired to Pennsylvania.

- Both their vice presidents and successors were southern Democrats named Johnson who were born in '08.

- Both presidents were concerned with the problems of black Americans and made their views strongly known in '63.

- Both presidents were shot in the head on a Friday in the presence of their wives.

- Both presidents were accompanied by another couple and the male companion of the other couple was wounded by the assassin.

- Lincoln was shot by John Wilkes Booth at Ford's Theatre; Kennedy was shot by Lee Harvey Oswald in a Lincoln automobile, made by Ford.

- Lincoln had a secretary named Kennedy who told him not to go to the theater; Kennedy had a secretary named Evelyn Lincoln who warned him not to go to Dallas.

- Both presidents' last names have seven letters.

- Both presidents have five syllables in their full name (which counts Kennedy's middle initial).

- There are six letters in each Johnson's first name.

- Booth ran from a theater to a warehouse; Oswald ran from a warehouse to a theater.

It is relatively easy to find seemingly meaningful patterns relating any two people or events, but such patterns rarely stand up to rigorous scrutiny. Much of the list has been debunked, some entries are outright falsehoods, and many are trite or forced (number of letters in people's names.) Some of the items are true, such as the year in which Lincoln and Kennedy were each elected president, but this is not so unusual given that presidential elections are held only every four years, and both started their political careers a hundred years apart. Some of the items are simply untrue; for instance, Lincoln never had a secretary named Kennedy.

Despite my skepticism about fluke lists such as this, I have found one remarkable similarity between Lincoln and Kennedy; it is too incredible to be mere happenstance. I'll add it to the list:

- Two years before his assassination, Lincoln was in Monroe, Maryland. Two years before his assassination, Kennedy was in Marilyn Monroe.

Mere coincidence? I think not.

▓ **Common sense**   Go out on a limb; that is where the fruit is.

Nonsense on Facebook

Facebook is a hotbed of foolish rumors and many are about Facebook itself. About once a month, I'll get an "insiders' tip" that Facebook is about to start charging for its services. The notice urges me to join them in petitioning Facebook to cease such a plan and let it know we will boycott the site if there is a charge.

So why is it obvious this is a hoax? First, if Facebook was to introduce an imminent charge to use their site, then, of course, they would say as much on their website as well as begin to prep its subscribers to the change. Also, the mainstream media websites would also report the story with bold headlines. Furthermore, such a change would not make sense for the company. Their business model depends on selling advertising to companies expecting mass distribution—sometimes in the hundreds of millions. If Facebook was to charge for subscriptions, the number of subscribers would drop astronomically. And the advertisers would dry up in a heartbeat. Another reason to ignore this message is simple: It has been circulating for years and it has yet to occur. When will we catch on?

Conspiracy Theories

A conspiracy theory is a belief that explains an event as the result of a secret plot by exceptionally powerful and cunning conspirators to achieve an evil end. The appeal of such theories is threefold: First, conspiracy theories claim to explain what institutional analysis cannot. They appear to make sense out of a world that is otherwise confusing. Second, they do so in an appealingly simple way, by dividing the world sharply between the forces of light and the forces of darkness. They trace all evil back to a single source, the conspirators and their agents. Third, conspiracy theories are often presented as special, secret knowledge unknown or unappreciated by others. For conspiracy theorists, the masses are a brainwashed herd whereas the conspiracy theorists in the know can congratulate themselves on penetrating the plotters' deceptions.

JFK's Assassination

JFK's assassination was the result of a conspiracy. Psychologists believe that the search for meaning is common in such theories and may be powerful enough alone to lead to the first formulation of the idea. Here is an example. Perhaps the greatest body on conspiracy theories centers around the assassination of President John F. Kennedy. Now, there is not enough space in this book to debunk all the dozens of conspiracy theories surrounding this horrid event,[3] but we should look at why such theories have erupted and spread. The sad fact is that we just cannot accept that a lone loser like Lee Harvey Oswald can take from us the most powerful man in the world. This act was a terrible wrong and caused such devastation to the hopes of a generation that we could not tolerate that it could have possibly been caused by a single individual. We can only accept such an event if we blame it on a powerful and sinister force, such as the mafia, the CIA, or the Soviet Union.

Sadly, history is ripe with a single person altering the course of humankind. We have to accept this unfortunate fact; if we can't, we have to create conspiracy fantasies.

The Clinton "Body Count"

Bill Clinton was quietly killing his associates. Individuals named by conspiracy theorists originated from a list of 34 suicides, accidental deaths, and unsolved murders prepared in 1993 by the pro-gun lobby group American Justice Federation, which was led by Linda Thompson. The conspiracy theory was further promulgated by a fund-raising documentary sold by Reverend Jerry Falwell. This silliness can be debunked easily by noting the following:

- Most of those claimed to be assassinated actually died from very well-documented accidents that leave no possibility of assassination.

- A political figure who becomes president of the United States will have a loosely defined circle of "associates," and many of these associates are in dangerous positions (police officers, pilots, soldiers) or older men in high-stress jobs (who are, therefore, at greater risk of dying of stress-related disease or suicide).

---

[3] Let me recommend a book that does debunk these many theories, one by one. Read *Case Closed* by Gerald Posner.

- And the definition of *associate* is so loose that pretty much anyone dying mysteriously can be somehow grouped with the president.

I can give you several reasons to dislike Bill Clinton, but master assassin just ain't one of them.

Common sense   A little common sense will stop a lot of divorces. Of course, it would stop a lot of marriages, too.

Water Fluoridation

Water fluoridation is a communist plot. Fluoridation is the controlled addition of fluoride to a public water supply to reduce tooth decay. Almost all major health and dental organizations support water fluoridation, or have found no association with adverse effects. Yet, when water fluoridation was introduced, great uproar resulted. I can well remember when fluoridation was debated in my hometown during the 1960s. It was the hot topic on radio talk shows, at backyard picnics, and even at church. The story seemed to be that fluoridation was a communist plot to destroy America. Seriously. Why our own government, from the president all the way down to local council members, wanted to destroy its citizens was never really explained. Another line of attack was that fluoridation actually caused teeth to rot and it was the dentists who were pushing the effort so they could make more money.

All this would be laughable if it wasn't for the fact that so many people believed it. So who benefitted from such a rumor? Actually, this triggered the start of the bottled water industry.[4]

"There Was No Holocaust"

The Holocaust was a hoax. Holocaust denial claims imply that the Holocaust is a hoax arising out of a deliberate Jewish conspiracy to advance the interest of Jews and to justify the creation of the State of Israel. For this reason, Holocaust denial is generally considered to be an anti-Semitic conspiracy theory.

---

[4]Oh geez, what have I done? Someone is going to quote me and claim that I said the bottled water industry was the source of the fluoride conspiracy theory. I may have just started my own conspiracy theory.

Unlike most of the conspiracy theories (explained later in this text) the motivation for spreading this hoax is just pure hate. The Holocaust is well documented by photos, film, victim testimony, as well as testimony from the Allied soldiers who rescued them. Such a hoax can be easily and convincingly debunked, if the listener has any inclination in doing so. The perpetrators of this ugly hoax have no interest in debunking it; their motivation is hate, pure and simple hate. And one thing they learned from Hitler is the effectiveness of the Big Lie. A lie is believable if you make it as big as possible and repeat it often enough.

The Pentagon Was Hit By a Missile on 9/11

The Pentagon was hit by a missile, not a plane, on 9/11. The evidence for this, say skeptics, is that the major damage to the building comprised a roundish blast hole, not the more extended destruction some say would be caused by airplane wings.

This theory ignores the considerable evidence of the bodies of passengers and crew at the site that were photographed. Thousands of people, including a friend of mine from high school, saw the plane fly into the Pentagon. Some quickly photographed the scene. Anyone planting plane debris at the site afterward would surely have been seen.

Twin Towers Felled by Demolition

The Twin Towers collapsed as a result of a controlled demolition, not from being struck by airplanes. Again, this ignores thousands of people who witnessed the planes hitting the towers, in addition to live TV coverage of the second strike. Besides, how do you get enough explosives—and place them in the exact spots necessary—without anyone noticing this considerable activity?

Common sense   Politicians and diapers should be changed regularly, and for the same reason.

The Latest Conspiracy Theory: Argo

The movie Argo was a conspiracy. Now Iran's state-run TV station is alleging that director Ben Affleck is, in fact, a covert agent in real life. It bases the claim on a story by 9/11 truther Kevin Barrett, who they quote as saying "If the makers of *Argo* are deposed under oath, they may be forced to reveal that their film . . . is a covert operation disguised as a movie." This is also the plot of the movie *Argo,* based on the 1979 attack on the U.S. embassy in Iran. And I thought all the loons were here in the United Sates.

Mr. and Mrs. Jesus

Jesus was married. Bible conspiracy theories posit that much of what is known about the Bible—in particular, the New Testament—is a deception. These theories make various claims, the most noteworthy of which is that Jesus really had a wife, Mary Magdalene. I'm not sure why this has become such a shattering theory. Many religious Christian scholars will tell you that even if this was true it really wouldn't affect His message or His role as a deity.Nonetheless, it is false and must be debunked.

How can I be so certain that Jesus was not married? Look at I Corinthians, Chapter 9. In this chapter, Paul contemplates whether it would be proper for him to take a wife. He asks rhetorically, "Why shouldn't I have the comfort of a wife, just as Peter and Timothy?" Did you catch that? The answer to our question is not in what Paul said, but in what he didn't say. Why did he only use a couple of disciples as examples? If he wanted to make an indisputable case for his right to marry, why didn't he simply say, "just as Jesus did?" If Jesus had married, Paul would have certainly known it and would have mentioned it in this monologue.

New Coke

The New Coke fiasco was deliberate. A theory claims that the Coca-Cola Company intentionally changed to an inferior formula with New Coke with the intent of driving up demand for their classic product, later reintroducing it for their financial gain. Donald Keough, President of Coca-Cola, replied to this theory: "The truth is, we're not that dumb, and we're not that smart."

Moon Landing? Really?

The Apollo moon landings were staged in a Hollywood movie studio. According to theorists, this was done either because they never happened or to conceal some aspect of the truth of the circumstances of the actual landing. This is easy to debunk. More than 140,000 people were involved in the *Apollo* space program. If it were a hoax, NASA would need to arrange cover stories for all of them, as well as find a way to keep all of them quiet. Furthermore, every member of Congress and other high officials, including three presidents, would have to be in on the deception. This may be possible, but it would be a whole lot easier just to send some guys to the moon.

HIV-Engendered Genocide

Western pharmaceutical companies add HIV to vaccines distributed in Third World countries. Some people feel that conspiracy theories are harmless. Unfortunately, there are conspiracy theories that have devastating consequences. There have been suggestions that HIV has been added to polio vaccines being distributed by the World Health Organization in Nigeria. So you think hoaxes, conspiracy theories, and legends are just a harmless activity? Consider this. Since these claims have been in existence, there has been a marked increase in the number of polio cases in the country, because Muslim clerics have urged parents not to have their children vaccinated. Because of a silly, harmless hoax, children are dying.

Why Do People Believe?

Right now you are asking yourself, "Why does anyone believe these preposterous stories? An ounce of common sense would dispel 95% of them!" Good question. Let's look at some of the features that make urban legends and conspiracy theories so palatable.

- The most convincing feature of an urban legend is how the story begins. "This happened to a friend of my sister's," the story will begin. Urban legends were always witnessed by a close associate or a friend of that trustworthy individual. Let's face it. You just can't argue with an opening like that; otherwise, you would appear to be questioning a family member's honesty. This leads us to a way to identify a fictitious legend quickly: It almost always comes from a friend of someone who can be absolutely trusted.

- "Life is so much more interesting with monsters in it," says Mikel J. Koven, a folklorist at the University of Wales. "It's the same with these legends. They're just good stories." Urban legends offer insight into our fears and the state of society. They're also good fun. Most are harmless, for sure, and serve to offer us somewhat personalized stories that bring home moral or ethical principles. The problem is, of course, those that actually case harm.Some stories cause great harm, such as The Kidney Heist, which caused a reduction in legitimate kidney donations, or McWorms, which led to a significant reduction in revenues for some restaurant chains (as well as a loss of wages for many workers).

- The abundance of conspiracy theories and legends surrounding 9/11, the war in Iraq, and Hurricane Katrina points to distrust in the government by a lot of people. Many legends and conspiracy theories are attempts to explain things in life that are unexplainable. Scientific phenomena (such as Bigfoot) or political happenings (the JFK assassination), among other things, are all attempts to make sense out of events that seem beyond comprehension. We do not like stories that have an incomplete ending. These legends and theories are an attempt to fill that vacuum.

- In addition, there is the fact that some people are open to accepting such stories. Many people are simply wired that way. People don't just latch on to a single legend or theory. If you believe one, you are probably open to accepting them all. There is a strong association between income and belief levels: the better-off are less likely to believe in conspiracy theories. Perhaps this can be attributed to education.

- These stories are so much easier to distribute today than in the past. Patrick Leman wrote in the *New Scientist* that belief in conspiracy theories is on the rise thanks to the distribution power of the Internet. Now, instead of whispering the latest theory in the ear of one person at a time, the rumormonger can blast it to thousands of people instantly on his or her Facebook page. The story is then re-sent by many of the person's friends and, before long, it attains viral status. We tend to accept information that we get from multiple sources, and this "re-Tweeting" easily serves that purpose.

- A major reason for spreading legends and especially conspiracy theories is that it gives tellers a sense of being in the know. They feel they are the smart people in the room. They have it all worked out—and if you don't believe them, they make you feel that you are naive. However, the biggest reason people latch on to such theories and legends is that these theories give people a sense of control. People hate randomness. Random acts represent a loss of control over your destiny. As a mechanism against that dread, it turns out that it's much easier to believe in a conspiracy. When you have someone to blame, it's not just randomness.

And here is an amazing fact about why conspiracy theories actually grow and expand as new evidence comes to light debunking the theory. For instance, with the so-called Climategate scandal, there were nine different investigations, all of which have exonerated the scientists involved, but the response from the people proposing this scandal was that those investigations were a whitewash. So the conspiracy theory began with the scientists being corrupt; now, not only is it them, but it's also all the major scientific organizations of the world that investigated them as well as the US government and her secret ally, the United Nations, that are corrupt. Any facts or attempt to discredit a conspiracy theory is perceived as further evidence the conspiracy exists. It's tough to argue with that logic.

Summary

This has been a brief journey through the misuse of the greatest invention of our lifetime. The Internet is capable of enriching us, educating us, and inspiring us. People have suddenly become writers and publishers, and their words can be literally broadcast to millions at the push of a button. There is great power in this, but also great hazard. Learn how to use this remarkable tool for all its potential blessings. Perhaps more important, learn how to identify its misuse. Your future, your education, and—as we've seen—some people's lives may depend on it.

Decisions, Decisions, Decisions

Making Good Ones

One of my favorite cartoons is from The Far Side. In it, a new arrival in Hell is being tormented by the devil. He is facing two doors—one marked *Damned If You Do* and the other labeled *Damned If You Don't*—while the devil impatiently demands that the newbie hurry up and make a decision.

We have to make decisions constantly. Hundreds of decisions. We have to decide what to have for breakfast, which shoes to wear, what route to drive to work, whether to enroll our kids in soccer, whether to take the stairs or the elevator, which movie to see, who to vote for. Every time you turn around, there is yet another decision to be made. And as we are shown via The Far Side, there is just no end to the decision-making process.

A Decision-Making Model

Common sense is often defined as the ability to make good decisions. So, we all get hundreds of opportunities each day to demonstrate our common sense—or lack thereof. Because most of these decisions are not made by instinct, we must rely on a thought process that promotes the selection of good choices. If we have a logical process, we are more apt to make logical choices. And good choices show good common sense.

Let's look at a simple, systematic way to do this. The system may look a bit cumbersome, and for most everyday decisions, it certainly is. However, *learn the process*. Although major decisions may take hours or even days to use the whole process in detail, you'll find that this same process can be abbreviated and used in just seconds to make routine, daily choices.

Step One: Seek Many Options

Every third Tuesday, I don my long white robes, let my beard grow out, climb up Kennesaw Mountain, and work my second job as a philosopher. Although there is little money to be made in this occupation, it does help fulfill my Maslow need for self-actualization.

Perhaps the most success I've had in this position has been in discovering the secret to a happy, productive life. "Life," I proclaim from the mountaintop, "is about having lots of good options." And so I use this book as an opportunity to add my own corollary to that philosophy: *Good decisions are rooted in having lots of good options.*

Many bad decisions—and displays of lousy common sense—come from the mouths of folks who think they only have one option available. Rarely, however, are we in a situation in which there is only one course of action or only one perspective to be espoused. To display good common sense, we must first collect our choices. With enough options, we have a much better chance of selecting a wise course of action.

■ **Tip** Having trouble making a decision? First survey all your options. To broaden the pool of possibilities, rewind through your past decisions for additional choices.

Your first step in choosing an option is simply to accept that you have several options from which to choose. Although, prima facie, it may appear there is only one course of action, you almost certainly have several. Step back and think outside the box if you have to, or ask friends to suggest options. As I have often philosophized: There's more than one way to skin a cat, assuming that is what you really want to do with a cat.

Here is an important way to collect lots of options: *reflect on your past decisions*. Good or bad, each previous decision teaches a lesson. And although it is valuable to learn from your mistakes, don't ignore your triumphs. Include all your similar experiences in your list of options. Don't necessarily discard not-so-good options you considered in the past. It's quite possible that some of the options that would not work in similar situations you faced previously would be good options for the event you are currently facing.

Then, make a list of these options. Don't evaluate these options at this point; just make your list. Brainstorm with vigor and write down *every* idea that comes to mind, no matter how silly it may seem. You can always cross it off the list later, but crazy ideas often evolve into brilliant ones. If you eliminate ideas too quickly, you are not allowing yourself the chance to see some of these silly options evolve into genius.

Please note, that these creative options are just a *base* for your decision making. If you end the process at this point and select an off-the-wall solution before it is evaluated and perfected, you will fall into the pit of Common Nonsense. And that would defeat the whole purpose of the process, wouldn't it?

Common sense   If you are paranoid long enough, sooner or later, you are going to be right.

Step Two: Evaluate the Options

Here is an interesting insight: we make our biggest mistakes (and utter the dumbest remarks) not when we are uncertain, but when we are completely sure of ourselves. It is when we feel rock-solid certain that we drop our guard, throw all caution to the wind, and get ourselves into some serious doo-doo.

No, you can't check out every assumption in perfect detail. There's not the time for it, nor is this task a credible use of your time. But, you can—regardless of how quickly a decision is needed—make a quick review of your options and imagine the consequences if those assumptions are incorrect. If time does allow, you may want to do a bit of digging and gather more information to fill in any holes in your knowledge base.

For those of you who tend to be a bit anal, make a chart. As part of this evaluation, list every possible outcome for each option you are considering. Label the potential outcome as positive or negative. You might even find it helpful to make a diagram to lay out every possibility visually.

For each possible scenario, decide whether the best possible outcome is worth accepting the risk of the worst possible outcome. If the worst possible outcome is completely unacceptable to you—meaning, you could never accept the consequences if it happened—then you shouldn't pursue that option.

Step Three: Consult Your Guts

Perhaps you see this step as one that disregards the previous steps. After all, if you are going to go with your gut anyway, why bother with all the option evaluation?

When I speak about going with your gut, I am advising you to go with an *educated* gut. Indeed, making a decision based solely on instinct is the quickest way to display Common Nonsense. Such decisions are founded on nothing but an initial emotion or are seeded in bumper sticker intellect. However, if you rely on your gut after educating yourself adequately on the various options and risks, then you are prone to make a decision that is not only wise, but reflects your values.

Let's understand what the gut represents. The reaction you feel when faced with an issue is simply the accumulation of a lifetime of experiences, values, and lessons learned. Although your brain follows a computerlike pattern to weigh all these factors and return a thought, your gut has already digested this information and returned a feeling. So, which organ should you follow? Both.

Let your brain educate your gut on the options, and your gut usually delivers the best, most commonsense answer. Although the brain alone delivers a good solution for the average Joe, a solution designed by the brain–gut team is custom designed to fit you.

Here is some advice for allowing your brain and gut to work together as an effective team: *trust your gut instincts only within your sphere of competency.*

Research has shown that we build pathways to the brain as we acquire experiences. These pathways kick in whenever we encounter a situation similar to one we had in the past. (This explains why star athletes repeat an action to build muscle memory.) It's smart to rely on your gut whenever you are dealing with a situation that is within your expertise. Your subconscious is taking more into consideration than your brain overtly realizes.

The US Army conducted a study to determine how people make decisions while under pressure and whether that process could be improved. The initial results were a bit surprising. It seemed that many who make life-or-death decisions do so without any real process whatsoever.

Note   Guts + Brain = Good decision

I do a lot of work with the local department of emergency services—the fire department, in particular. We had an incident several years ago that underscores the value of following your gut. An engine company responded to what was initially a rather routine call—a kitchen fire. While his team was hosing the fire, the lieutenant got an uneasy gut feeling and ordered all the firefighters out of the house immediately. The floor collapsed just as the men cleared the building. If they had not left when they did, the entire team would have been killed in the fire that was raging in the basement below.

The lieutenant claimed his decision was based on nothing more than a gut feeling. However, later investigation showed that there were some factors present that gave rise to his sixth sense. The fire was much hotter than a routine kitchen fire. The flames were not responding to the water and, perhaps most eerie, the scene was just "too quiet." Everything was out of place for it to be a routine kitchen fire scenario, and this is what instigated the lieutenant's intuition. (The fact was, the fire originated in the basement, not the kitchen appliances.) This gut feeling was formed because the situation violated the firefighter's previous experiences with kitchen fires. His sixth sense wasn't instinct; it was learned through responding to hundreds of kitchen fires during his career. His gut had been well educated.

Perhaps you are nodding your head at the idea of using your gut to make good commonsense decisions, but are not exactly sure how to do this. You might ask, "How can I tell what my gut is saying?" Here are some ideas:

- *Go with your first instinct.* Your gut is usually the first one to speak.

- *If you find that you are talking yourself into something, your gut is telling you that it is not a good decision.* Good decisions usually feel right.

- *Think of your role models and heroes—the people who inspire you.* What would they do in your place and why? This method has become a popular decision guide for many Christians who wear bracelets that bear the question *What would Jesus do?*

- *Contemplate the options and select the one you feel a sense of excitement for.* Consider whether you will be able to look proudly into the mirror the next day.

- *Use my wife's method.* My wife has a similar litmus test for decision making. She simply reviews the options and goes with the one that gives her peace. Frankly, that's probably the sanest way to make decisions reflecting common sense.

Common sense   Don't learn the tricks of the trade. Learn the trade.

Step Four: Make a Choice

This is, of course, the object of the whole exercise. Hopefully, there is a decision on your list that is backed up by both your brain and your gut. If not, then you probably need to go back to the first step and search for more options, then do more research into those options. The fact is, one of these new options—or one you have already surveyed—may be the right course for you. You might not have realized this because you didn't looked closely enough at the details of the option. Your brain just hasn't been tickled adequately.

Or, perhaps it is your gut that has not been properly stimulated. Or, maybe your gut does have an opinion but you've done a lousy job of listening. Here's how you can be a better gut-listener: flip a coin. If, while that coin is in midair, you find yourself hoping it comes out one way, you have your answer. Or if, after seeing the result, you wish it had come out differently, you also have your answer.

I just love including sophisticated scientific processes in my programs.

Step Five: Verbalize

It's a good idea to talk through your decision-making process with another person. When the thought process is internalized, we can sometimes skip over obvious choices. By talking with another person, any irrational thoughts or faulty logic can often be uncovered. I learned this the hard way from one of the worst decisions I ever made. Not only was the decision bad, it was morally corrupt.

A district manager came to me and outlined a dilemma. A routine audit had uncovered that his best manager (Bob) had been altering timecards and shortchanging his employees on their paychecks. I thought for a moment and analyzed the situation. I remembered I had been putting great pressure on the teams to deliver excellent labor numbers and that probably pushed the manager to take some shortcuts. "I'll tell you what," I said to the district manager. "Sit Bob down and take him to within an inch of his life. Have him make an apology to the crew and reimburse them for what he shortchanged them." I sent the district manager on his way, proud of my decision that took care of the employees while saving a good manager.

My boss caught wind of the situation and invited me into his office for a "personal development opportunity." "Ken, how about you talking me through your decision-making process on this one," Dale quietly requested.

I began explaining how I reached my decision. I was halfway through the second sentence when I heard what I was saying. I was shocked. I interrupted myself to say, "Holy smoke!"[1] I am absolutely wrong. I can't believe I made a decision like that." Dale nodded, knowing he'd just taken me through a learning experience.

I personally fired the manager and apologized to the employees. Reimbursements were distributed, in cash, immediately. Although I eventually corrected the situation, I still kick myself for my initial corrupt decision—a decision that could have been avoided if I had only talked through my thoughts before making the decision.

Step Six: Do It!

When the choices and decisions get to be too much, what do we do? Most of us procrastinate. Instead of making a choice, we set it aside and let it fester. The number of things that need deciding tend to pile up rather quickly. Soon, instead of having to make one decision, we have to make five. Or ten. Or 50. By doing nothing, we have forfeited any claim to basic common sense.

Recognize that indecision is a decision in itself. It is the decision to do nothing, which might be the worst decision of all. But don't get lost in the decision-making process, either. Give yourself a time limit if you have to make the decision soon or if the decision is relatively unimportant. After you have made a decision, implement it completely. Remember these words from your now-favorite guru: *A pretty good decision implemented quickly is far superior to a perfect decision that you never quite got around to implementing.*

---

[1] Or words to that effect.

Last, don't look back. At this stage, don't be confused by thinking about the other potential alternatives that you did not pick. Yes, this means you will make some mistakes. Fortunately, it is rare that any one decision will determine your fate. The fact is, any decision you reach using this simple evaluation method yields an action that—at the very least—displays some pretty good common sense. Even if it is not the most brilliant course of action ever devised, it will most certainly be viewed as one that displays some solid common sense.

NAPOLEON'S (NON)DECISION-MAKING PROCESS

Ralph Waldo Emerson wrote, about Napoleon Bonaparte, "It was a whimsical economy of the same kind which dictated his practice, when general in Italy, in regard to his burdensome correspondence. He directed Bourrienne to leave all letters unopened for three weeks, and then observed with satisfaction how large a part of the correspondence had thus disposed of itself and no longer required an answer."

You're not Napoleon, so you might have trouble explaining to your boss why you didn't answer his e-mail asking for a decision from three weeks ago, but Napoleon was on to something. Sometimes, the right decision is to do nothing. Situations have a way of resolving themselves, and making a quick decision to *do something* sometimes interferes with the group and its efforts to solve a problem.

Then again, Napoleon also said, "Take time to deliberate, but when the time for action comes, stop thinking and go in."

On the Other Hand . . .

After reading this chapter, you might become convinced that good common sense demands that you produce decisions at a machine gun pace. Often, this is the case. As I previously stated, indecision is a decision in itself, and I am not backing off from that advice when I deliver this one final gem: sometimes the best decision is to do nothing.

Here is a great perspective from former *Apollo* astronaut Captain Alan Bean. Test pilots are quite experienced in dealing with problems and making quick decisions (and those decisions are literally life-or-death choices). Pilots have developed a litmus test when evaluating such problems. When something is amiss, they first ask themselves this central question: Is this thing still flying? If the answer is yes, they realize there is no immediate problem and certainly no need for panicked decision making. There is nothing pushing them to overreact, which would create a whole new set of problems.

Tip Ask yourself: Is the plane still flying? If it is, then you have time to make a sensible decision.

Captain Bean recalls when his *Apollo 12* spacecraft was hit by lightning. Lights flashed, bells sounded, and the capsule shook. All these things created incredible tension and excitement; there was strong temptation to *just do something*! But instead of flailing for solutions, the pilots simply asked themselves, "Is this thing still flying in the right direction?" Well, as a matter of fact, it was. Despite the drama, the spacecraft was still headed for the moon. So the pilots let the lights glow, and the bells and whistles do their thing while they calmly addressed each problem. As they did so, they watched the red lights blink out one by one. The loud alarms quieted as they went about solving the individual issues. Eventually, all was calm and the mission proceeded without further crisis.

Captain Bean gives us commonsense decision advice about how to face a pressure-packed crisis. "If your thing is still flying, think first and then act."

A Supplemental System: Let Others Make Decisions for You

Of course, most of the decisions we make don't require a lot of detailed analysis. The steady stream of decisions we face are usually rather cut-and-dried choices that require minimal analysis. Then again, we often seem to have a cascade of conundrums that calls for deep analysis, usually in areas in which we have no experience. However, even though the situation is significant and the knowledge gap may be huge, who has the energy to conduct such research on a regular basis? Isn't there a system for making good commonsense decisions without such hard work? Yep. Do what I do. Whenever possible, I let others do the thinking for me.

When I am faced with a big decision or problem, I remind myself that I'm almost certainly not the first person to have faced such an issue. In fact, I doubt I have *ever* been faced with a unique problem. So, rather than going through all the steps and research, and sweating blood that comes from having to make a decision, I just look at how others have solved the problem successfully. This makes me look like a genius.

Hey, why reinvent the wheel?

Summary

A characteristic of a person with common sense is his or her ability to make good, solid decisions. The ability to make good decisions is not something you are born with (as every parent can confirm); it is developed. Use these ideas to develop this skill and watch your reputation for rationality grow.

Now we have gotten a good framework for making solid decisions, let's explore how you can use this common sense skill in the workplace.

Commonsense Behavior in the Office

I offer a monthly workshop assisting unemployed Boomers. A key part of the workshop is giving them the secret for acing an employment interview. They learn this secret by while we all sing a rousing version of The Barney Song. Yep, the purple dinosaur pretty well covers it all. The paraphrased lyrics:

> I like you.
>
> You like me.
>
> We're a happy family

Perhaps I should explain (while you attempt to get that damn tune out of your head). When you are invited to an interview, the company has already determined you are qualified for the job. Credentials are no longer the issue. What they want to discover at this point is whether the relationship is a good fit. There are three questions to be answered to determine this. Do we like you? Do you like us? And are you like everyone else around here?

This may seem a bit shallow to you, but if you think about it, it makes a lot of sense. In my rather extensive management career, I have, regrettably, discharged or approved the termination of many dozens of people. Rarely was one of these terminations caused by a lack of qualifications or job performance. It just was not an issue. The second-most reason for termination was integrity issues. The oft-most? Inability to get along with coworkers (or customers).

Some people call it *manners*. Some refer to it as *keeping your nose clean*. Some call it *navigating the waters*. Others bluntly call it *office politics*. I just think of it as showing common sense around the office.

Let's look at some of the commonsense actions you need to display at work. You may be surprised at how such basic actions and attitudes can combine to propel your career—or at least help you hang on to your job while everyone else is getting laid off.

Common Sense Self-Behavior

The first application of common sense principles has to do with how you perceive your place in the workplace.

Think of Yourself as a Problem Solver

How many times have you heard someone say, "I could have gotten it done, but a problem got in the way?" Workers deficient in common sense consider it adequate merely to explain why they didn't get the job done. People who build great careers understand that the only reason anyone is ever hired is to solve problems.

Tip   Never make excuses for why something didn't get done, no matter the reason. Your job is to solve problems.

Develop Resilience

A great bumper sticker from the 1990s (text slightly modified): STUFF HAPPENS. Look, bad things really do happen to good people. Have an even-tempered response to unfair comments, derailed suggestions, and business crises. This is common sense for a reason: There is a firm dividing line between people who become enormous successes in life and those who eventually lay around in an alley drinking Woolite. This is not to say that successful people never have setbacks. (Actually, they tend to have numerous and vivid career disasters.) No, those who succeed face great hurdles; they've just learned to pick themselves up and attack one more time.

Those around you observe how you react to setbacks. If you panic and are short-tempered, you will find that your reputation and effectiveness will erode. People notice who stays calm in battle and who keeps their head when others are losing theirs. Pick yourself up, brush yourself off, and move on.

Take the Blame

Taking the blame for a failure can be a strong way to enhance your role in your company, because whoever accepts the blame for a failure will eventually get credit for that project's eventual success. Declaring yourself responsible for failure also brands you as a person who accepts responsibility. Look for opportunities to take this responsibility; these are most easily found during the darkest days.

■ **Common sense**   There is nobility in service.

Volunteer for Unpleasant Tasks

Have you every cleaned out the office refrigerator? If the copier is jammed, do you fix it? How do you address an empty coffee pot or a burned-out light bulb? Every office has a small core of workers who do all the unpleasant or undesirable work. Join them. Very few folks *want* to do these things, but they are relatively easy tasks, and they genuinely help your coworkers. You'll build up additional capital in the bank of goodwill you can draw upon later.

Be a Peer Leader

For most of the 1980s, my Atlanta Braves were abysmal. This was not the case in 1982, however, when the team actually made the playoffs. The team was on the plane home when they received word of their accomplishment. The Giants had just beat the Dodgers, thus giving the Braves the Western Division Championship by the slimmest of margins: one single game.

Amid the celebration, Dale Murphy sat quietly. Murphy had been the National League Most Valuable Player for two consecutive years and was probably the best player in the game at the time. If anyone deserved the credit for the championship, it was Dale Murphy, which made the next thing he did remarkable.

Murphy moved from seat to seat, holding brief conversations with each of his teammates. "Hey, Ted," he would say. "Do you remember that catch you made that saved two runs and let us win the Expos game? That's the game we won the division by." Then he'd move over and say to Bob, "Remember the home run you hit to beat the Mets in April? That's the game we won the division by." And he continued this, speaking with each player—star and benchwarmer alike—reminding him of one thing he did that allowed the team to win one game during the season. And that was always the one game that won the division championship.

Dale Murphy didn't own the team, and he was not a manager. Nope, he was someone far more important. He was a peer leader.

Many people misunderstand the meaning of peer leadership. Some think it means to act as a pseudo boss, ordering people around without the benefit of real authority. However, leadership has nothing to do with management. Although management is a formal, structural arrangement, leadership is a trait that can be exhibited by anyone in the organization. Unlike being the boss, everyone can be a peer leader. Demonstrate peer leadership within your group and you will see your value in the organization soar, and your reputation for common sense propel your career.

Note   Leadership isn't about "being the boss." The mail room clerk sometimes shows more leadership ability than the CEO. Leadership is the ability to rally your team and set a direction through influence instead of power.

Commonsense Behavior with Coworkers

There are some commonsense principles you will want to incorporate in your behavior toward your fellow coworkers. The first deals with whom you choose to associate.

Pick Your Flock

The animal kingdom has taught us an important business truth: Birds of a feather flock together. The fact is, you will be perceived in the same image as those with whom you associate, and your work output will also reflect theirs. This is both good news and bad news. On the one hand, it is easy to associate with the wrong crowd; they actually recruit members. Gathered around the coffeepot or in the corner of the lunchroom, these people are barely hanging on to their jobs, and they use every breath to gripe, back-stab, and complain. They will try to draw you in to their nattering network of negativism. Walk briskly away from destructive people.

On the other hand, you can be considered someone on the fast track just by being associated with those who actually are. This is also easy to do. These blessed people are eager to include you in their network. Just schedule lunch appointments with the Golden People on a regular basis and get to know them. You will adopt their image by osmosis.

You become your environment. You will reflect the same standards, level of success, and image of the people and situations you choose to be around. This is a case that goes beyond the concept of "perception is reality"—perception *becomes* reality.

Tip   It's very easy to join the "bad guys" tribe at work. They always want more people to complain to, and they'll make you feel good when you blast other people. But it's also easy, if a little more work, to join the fast trackers by speaking with them often and emulating their best traits.

Remember People

Many companies and corporate cultures grow cold and impersonal. People are often treated similar to paperclips and they just don't like it. You will be amazed at the loyalty you can accumulate if you treat people like, well, people, in your interactions with them. There are just a couple basic things you need to do to generate solid, loyal relationships. First, and as mentioned earlier in this book, remember names. This is a real trick for some people. In fact, I know a gentleman who proudly declares, "You know how some people will say, 'I can't remember your name but I never forget a face?' Well, I can't remember faces either." There are several great methods available that teach you how to remember names. Pick one and master it. The method I use is pretty simple: Just listen to the person's name when introduced. It's amazing how our minds wander during an introduction. We are trying to think about what we are going to say next instead of hearing the person. When introduced, listen to the name as it is being said. Repeat the name several times, for instance respond simply with, "It's great to meet you, [Jim Simpson]!" This will implant the name in your brain.

There is nothing that sounds more beautiful to someone than the sound of their own name. Likewise, there is no greater slight than a coworker not knowing your name, getting it mangled, or even more insulting, being referred to as, "Hey fella!"

Knowing people's names is so very basic, but you can quickly take this to a much higher level. The only music sweeter than hearing your own name is to be asked about your spawn. Occasionally inquire about coworkers' children when making small talk. Now don't simply say, "How are your kids doing?" That's not particularly impactful. Much stronger would be, "How's Bubba, Jr., doing in Little League this summer? Has he hit one out of the park yet?" or "Let's see now, Allison's been attending Auburn for a full semester now. How does she like college life?" This type of attention moves you from being simply a nice coworker to a good personal friend. People tend to look after their friends.

Be a Team Player

We Americans pride ourselves on being individuals. It's good to have a personal identity and not be a clone. However, to your coworkers, you must be known as a member of the team, someone working toward the good of the organization rather than personal glory. You must be perceived as a team player.

Team players are those who help the team achieve its goals, help other people achieve their goals, and who evaluate their performance on the success of the entire group. Personal victories should be publicized as team victories. Even if you had a personal victory, any team setback should be treated as a personal loss. Let me explain this one. Suppose you just recorded excellent sales for the third quarter. Unfortunately, no other member of the sales team did well and your division missed its plan by 15%. Your attitude should be concern over the team loss, not excitement for your personal victory.

Common sense   "You can't build a reputation on what you are going to do." —Henry Ford

---

Don't Be This Person

This is an appropriate place to address an American phenomenon: the devil's advocate. There really are some people who think they are building a reputation for competence by constantly playing the devil's advocate role. You know the people I'm talking about. A workgroup will, for example, hear of a potential problem-solving program in a meeting and, before it can be brainstormed, Mr. No[1] leans back in his chair, cocks his head to one side, and mews out those loathsome words: "Let me play the devil's advocate for a moment." Understand what is actually going on. Mr. No is not about to engage in a constructive examination of factors that may need tweaking. No, instead he is using the tactic of ripping apart the good intentions of others while hiding behind a useful role. It's his way of eviscerating others while hiding behind a façade.

Devil's advocates, even when they make legitimate points, are not popular people. Their actions are counter to the concept of teamwork and are an antithesis to an individual's role on the team. Do this more than once and you will gain the reputation of an outsider. You will be avoided and not invited to meetings or informal gatherings. You will have earned a reputation as someone who cannot work and play with others.

Tip   It might seem to be a good idea to play devil's advocate, but if that becomes your persona at work, people will avoid you, and your career will go nowhere.

Compliment Liberally

Help your teammates feel good about themselves. You can do this by paying compliments. You should be liberal with your compliments, but you should make them in such a way that it doesn't border on brownnosing. Here is how you can make lots of ally-building compliments without creating the reputation of being a pure suck-up:

- Only compliment people when you absolutely believe what you are saying. Insincere compliments always come across as insincere. Worse yet, you sound sarcastic. That's the opposite impression you want to make.

- Compliment people behind their back. When chatting with your teammate's best friend, mention that it looks like Harry has lost a few pounds, or that Martha's report was the best you have read in a long time. Your kind words will get back to them, and will have significantly greater impact than if you paid them the compliment to their face.

---

[1] Not his real name

- Compliment the act, not the person. "This report is outstanding!" carries much more punch than, "You wrote an outstanding report!" Commenting on the act also allows you to go into much more detail and use more superlatives than if you comment about the person directly.

- Include your boss in your complimentary campaign, although here is where you should most certainly do so behind her back. Say good things about your boss to her boss. It is difficult to tell your boss that she did a great job on something without appearing to be a pathetic yes-person. Wait for the opportunity to mention it to her boss. Now you have scored two points—one with your boss and another with the boss's boss, who will note that you are a loyal person and a valued direct report.

Commonsense Relationships with Your Boss

You should obey your boss. Sounds pretty basic, I know. The revelation here, however, is not that you should obey your boss—it's the reason *why* you should obey her. As with all other important aspects of life, this principle can be illustrated by a baseball story.

Few managers were better strategists than Earl Weaver—a brilliant baseball mind, no doubt. He was blessed with some great players on his team, and among them was future Hall of Famer Reggie Jackson. Reggie was not only a great player, but he possessed one of the game's healthiest egos. Conflict was inevitable.

Weaver knew he was a strategy genius, so it was not surprising he controlled every aspect of the game. For instance, no one was allowed to steal a base without his permission. This rule was accepted by most players, but Reggie found it to be an affront. After all, he was a perennial all-star and had a 90% success rate on swiping second. Maybe the other players needed such close supervision, he reasoned, but the Great Reggie Jackson needed no such oversight.

Reggie decided to prove his point during the second game of an important double-header. Without his skipper's approval, Reggie broke for second. He stole the base easily. In fact, the catcher didn't even make a throw. Reggie gave the dugout a smirk as he glanced at Weaver, who had thrown his hat to the ground and was shouting many of the seven words that cannot be said on television. Reggie figured the manager's behavior was just a product of a bruised ego, and he rather enjoyed the moment.

In the clubhouse after the game, tempers had tempered. Weaver decided to have a teaching moment with Reggie. He explained that the next batter was Lee May, currently the team's hottest hitter. First base came open when Reggie trotted to second, so the pitcher simply walked May. This took the bat out of the hands of Baltimore's best batter. The next scheduled batter had never been able to hit this particular pitcher, so Weaver was forced to pinch hit for him.

Thus, the pinch hitter was not available later in the game when he was desperately needed. The Orioles could not take advantage of the opportunity that presented itself in the ninth inning and the team lost a game they could have won.

First, understand the point I am not making. I am not saying, obey your boss because he knows more about your job than you do. Actually, I'm pretty sure he doesn't; I'm sure you know far more about your job than your boss does—just as I am certain Reggie Jackson knew much more about being a baseball player than Earl Weaver did.

But if that's not my point, what is? Here is why you should obey your boss: he is looking at a bigger picture than you are and is attempting to direct your expertise to be the most useful into the overall strategy.

Reggie's job was to run the bases. Weaver's job was to win ballgames. And that is why you should obey your boss.

Help Your Boss Help You Help Her to Help You

I still feel amazement when I think about a district manager I once had working for me. We'll call him Skippy. Skippy was a reasonably competent individual, not extraordinary by any means, but adequate. As with most of us, his performance needed to be improved in a few areas and I had tried to work with him to do just that. But, no matter how much effort I put in, Skippy's performance seemed just to stay in place.

I always had an uneasy feeling when I was with him. I couldn't quite put my finger on it, but our relationship certainly featured a stonewall. After much digging, I finally understood why. He let me know that he didn't like me personally. I'm a sensitive kind of guy and that stung. We held hands and sang a few verses of "Kumbaya," and then I explained to him that regardless of our lack of deep personal bonding, his performance did need to improve, and that I would do all I could to help him work to his potential.

In several meetings, I left no doubt that I could be of enormous help in his personal development. At the very least, I could show him how to save his career. Word got back to me from several sources that his attitude seemed to be that he was more interested in slamming me than in promoting himself. He didn't stay employed much longer.

So what's the point of this little story? My point is that, as idiotic as this man's actions were, they are not all that uncommon. Look around your office and you'll find a few Skippys. These are people who look upon the boss as the enemy rather than the coach.

Long story short: He rejected my help. Not only did he not embrace my assistance, he became downright hostile. Rather than working on the areas I had outlined, he seemed to spend any commonsense genes approaching me as his enemy. (It was almost as if he thought if he could outargue me, he would "win." Not unlike a teenager, frankly.)

Don't do this. Instead, look upon your boss as the team captain or—better yet—your coach. So, why should you approach your boss in such a positive manner? Is it because you want to build a rah-rah atmosphere and see beautiful daisies sprouting from the baseboards? (Cue the music . . . Partridge Family sings "Sunshine, Lollypops, and Rainbows.") Actually, as wonderful as this paradigm might first seem, this is not why you wrap your arms around your boss. You do it for selfish reasons. It is in your own best interest.

■ **Tip** Don't fight your boss. You won't win. If you truly don't like your boss, look for another job. (In fact, "Don't like my boss" is the leading cause of people quitting a job.)

Never Surprise Your Boss

Some surprises can be great fun, but surprising your boss will not bring a smile to her face. Bosses are expected to know what you are doing, and they get labeled incompetent by their boss if they don't know what you are working on. Although there is great drama involved in surprising your boss with a piece of quality work, the pleasure she gets from seeing an unexpected gain is overshadowed by her fear of not knowing what else you are up to. Surprises make the boss feel like things are out of control, even when good things are happening. Keep the boss informed. You'll lose the fun of the surprise, but the relationship will benefit in the long run.

Commonsense Relationships with Your Customers

The commonsense technique in dealing with customers is simply this: Listen to them. You will be shocked to see how effectively this behavior works in dealing with client issues. Here are two examples.

Heather Howard of New Orleans used this tactic in solving a difficult issue with a client. Heather recounts:

> For about 10 years, I worked as a writer/producer/ editor for a small, family-owned video production company. We had a client that I liked to call "our favorite customer and least-favorite customer rolled into one." "Favorite" because he paid his bills on time. "Least favorite" because he was extremely cheap and very picky! He supplied his own used tape stock for commercial production and never wanted to pay more than $150 for any job (the cost of one hour of editing). However, he always had very specific—often complicated—ideas of how the jobs should be done. Our company did not have a graphic artist on staff. We had an excellent artist that we could outsource to, but that cost money. For this man, I was forced to muddle through using my own rudimentary graphics skills.
>
> For one commercial, he gave me a photo of a model wearing a sports coat that his store was selling. The image needed to be scanned, then cut out and placed over a different background. I struggled to figure out how I was going to do this with my extremely limited PhotoShop skills. I finally had to admit that the task was beyond me and the image was too detailed for me to cut out cleanly. My client reaches into his briefcase and pulls out the same image that he had hand-cut out of the background with scissors and says, "I don't guess you can just use this one, can you?"

> I was flabbergasted. In this age of computer graph-
> ics and digital everything, cutting out an image with
> scissors and scanning it without the background
> had never occurred to me! It was exactly what we
> needed and it looked just fine. Thanks to my crazy
> client's common sense, we finished the commercial
> on time and under budget!

I adopted this philosophy of "Ask the Customer" many years ago when addressing the issue of dealing with customer complaints. The fast-food industry, because of the thousands of daily transactions and the dozens of independent actions for each of these transactions, sees an unusual number of errors. Mistakes are plentiful and customer complaints are inevitable.

Every company has developed its approach and plans for dealing with these mistakes. Most have matrices that show the response to be made for each particular transgression. Many companies even require various levels of approval just to ensure the company is responding to the complaint in the best possible reflection of customer service.

I took a different, simpler approach. I found the best way to satisfy customers is to ask them what they want and give it to them immediately. No paperwork, no deep analysis, no judgment. Whenever I received a negative comment card or phone complaint from customer, I would apologize, express my disappointment, and ask, "What can I do to make this right?" Note that I could be confident that I always did the right thing. This is because I gave customers exactly what they asked for.

I carried this philosophy to the lowest possible level in the restaurant. Even if a dining room attendant was working his first day on the job, each employee was authorized to fix any mistake. The first thing new employees learned how to say was, "I'm sorry. I'll fix this right away."

Commonsense customer service: Listen to the customer.

Commonsense Office Politics

This will be a short section. Politics is usually a dirty and complicated subject, but it really shouldn't be. Office politics is nothing more than developing relationships with others. Some people go about this in a nasty, intimidating fashion, and this does work sometimes, at least temporarily. But eventually, this J.R. Ewing approach comes back to bite them; you can barely hear the sound of their implosion because of the sound of champagne corks popping.

There's only one "game" you should play with your coworkers. It's the world's strongest political tactic. This is a political move I learned early in my career, and it has served me well. Heed these words: *Embrace the defeated.*

I learned this lesson from Senator Everett Dirkson, the minority leader of the Senate during Lyndon Johnson's presidency. Whenever there was a vote taking place in which his individual vote would make no difference, he would cast his lot with the side that was about to be soundly defeated. According to Dirkson, "The victors never remember and the defeated never forget." He found that later, when he needed to scare up some votes to get a bill passed, he could turn to some of those people he previously voted for on the losing side. They would remember that he had once stood by them and were eager to repay his kindness.

I once attended a monthly senior management breakfast meeting with the company president. I arrived at the front door to the restaurant at the same time as "Jack." Jack was the vice president of finance and had just been notified that he was being terminated at the end of the month. Jack looked at me and said half-jokingly, "You'd better wait here a minute. You don't want to be seen walking in with me." I looked him in the eye and said, "I am proud to be seen walking next to you." His eyes teared up as he felt respected for the first time in the past twenty-four hours. Not surprisingly, Jack remains a loyal business ally today.

Make it a point to befriend the peer who was chewed out at a meeting, or the person who was just forced to resign, or anyone having any type of career difficulty. These people will rise again, your paths will cross, and they will always remember your kindness.

And that's all you need to know about playing commonsense office politics.

Tip Office politics often come down to good manners or a lack of them. Use good manners in the office and you'll find the doors of opportunity opening on a continuous basis.

Summary

So much of your potential success or failure depends on how you can relate to your boss, peers, and subordinates. To relate well, you really don't need deep talent or a degree in psychology. You can deal with the folks in your office just by practicing a little common sense in your relationships.

We've seen just how critical it is to practice good common sense in the workplace. But right now you may be saying, "Of course we should use common sense in the workplace! But my problem is not convincing my employees to use it, it's getting them to possess it. How can I teach my team how to get some common sense?"

Good question. Some actionable answers are in the next chapter.

Teaching Common Sense in the Workplace

Or Learning It

In Chapter 2, we learned there are two types of intelligence—common sense and book smarts—which presents an interesting challenge for this particular chapter. We are learning common sense from a book. Does learning common sense from a book make it book smarts? An ethicist might characterize this conundrum as hypocrisy. However, if you will forgive this philosophical faux pas, we'll use this chapter to outline a few methods you can use to teach your employees to improve their common sense.

The Best Way to Learn

June: I thought Beaver had enough common sense to know he would get caught.

Ward: Maybe getting caught is how you get common sense.

—From *Leave It to Beaver*

There are four words that succinctly summarize the best way to learn common sense. These four words are:

Learn from your mistakes.

No magic here. These words not only describe how to learn common sense, but also indicate the essence of what common sense really is. Common sense understands life and how it all fits together. We learn this by bumping into walls, getting our nose bloodied, and knowing not to bump into that wall again. People who lack common sense never seem to grasp this. They go through life repeating the same mistakes and following the same flawed decision-making processes; it never occurs to them there may be other ways to get around the wall. People with great common sense still walk into walls. They just don't walk into the same wall—or similar walls—twice.

Want to take it a step further? You can polish your students' common sense education by helping them get their PhD in common sense, which can be accomplished by heeding these six words:

Learn from the mistakes of others.

Here are some ideas for teaching—and learning—common sense. Some are conventional, some are a bit novel, but all are based on the principle that you need to learn from your mistakes and learn from the mistakes of others.

Formalize Common Sense as a Goal

Perhaps the first step in teaching common sense is to make it clear this is a trait your employees must develop. Get the employees to understand that you expect them to develop this skill just as you expect them to learn other job skills, such as effective writing, interacting with people, or mastering a new computer program. How can you communicate this? Use the same method you communicate other required developments. Make it a part of employees' annual review.

Set aside time during employees' annual review to evaluate their grasp of commonsense issues. Have examples of their use (or lack thereof) of common sense in the workplace. Just as you do with other skills, review their successes and failures, and walk them through any missed opportunities for exhibiting good common sense. Make it clear that you consider this a topic they need to work on during the coming year, and outline ways they can learn or expand their acquisition of common sense—just as you would for any other job skill that needs development.

Agreed, this conversation does not flow as easily as it would if you are telling employees you want them to work on their writing, people, or any other job skills. It's not easy to tell people they are deficient in common sense. Perhaps this is one of those rare moments when kind deception may be morally permissible. So instead of saying, "Fred, I'm concerned about your lack of common sense, and it needs to be improved"; say this, instead:

> Fred,[1] I've always thought you usually display pretty good judgment; in fact, this may become a real strength if you work on it. And what a huge strength it would be; it could really propel your career in management. So here's what I want you to do: I want you to make it your personal development object this year to build up your judgment, decision-making skills, and common sense.

Does this sound a bit disingenuous to you? I understand. When giving performance feedback, I prefer to be brutally direct with folks. But, I fear that telling employees, "You ain't got no common sense," might alienate them from the process of acquiring it. This sample dialog is just a suggestion on how to introduce a sensitive deficiency; use your acquired people skills to create and use an effective method with which you are comfortable.

Regardless of how you introduce the topic, the point is to address common sense directly and in an organized fashion. Common sense is a job skill just as critical as any other skill or personal trait and should be developed. This chapter is designed to help you create targeted training in common sense. We introduce a few conventional methods for educating employees about this topic, but you just might find it is the unconventional approaches that are most effective.

Tip Recognize that common sense is a job skill just as critical as any other skill or personal trait.

---

[1] Call him Fred only if his name is Fred. If not, use his own name.

Hold Regular Discussions

Have employees keep a running list of decisions they have made, options they had to choose from, and the choice they finally made. Meet with employees regularly—ideally, weekly—and review their list. No, there is nothing novel about the approach I am suggesting. In fact, the chances of employees providing a very thorough list are low. So why do it? Two reasons: First, having regular meetings reinforces that commonsense development is an issue. If employees knows they'll be meeting with the boss regularly, they'll keep the issue in mind as well as put a bit more thought into the decisions they make. After all, if they have any common sense at all, they'll want to have an impressive list to show you at your meeting. (This requirement forces your employees to think through decisions and actions. Sometimes, common sense can be improved exponentially just by thinking before we act.) Second, regular meetings force regular discussions. People learn by talking through situations and hearing the analysis others can provide. ("Here's how I would have handled that ....")

Observe and Coach

A great way to teach common sense is to catch someone in the act of doing something stup—uh, lacking in common sense and then use it as a teaching moment. However, you don't really want to "catch" them or attack them. You'll scare them off and lose an opportunity to instill some wisdom and gain more useful employees.

A friend of mine once had an employee who graduated at the top of the class at a prominent university. Yes, he was valedictorian and had book smarts galore, but he lacked all common sense.

Once, when a company car was broken down by the side of the highway, he somehow got the idea that because the car wouldn't start, it might be low on oil. So he took off his shoe and then his (white) sock, pulled out the dipstick, and cleaned it off with his sock. He stuck the dipstick in, pulled it out, and saw that he had plenty of oil. So he put his sock and shoe back on, and pondered some more.

My friend wasn't able to help him in that situation—you either know not to use your socks to check your oil or you don't—but he offered numerous other opportunities to teach a lesson or two.

Another opportunity came along swiftly, of course. The employee got into a computer program used to run the business. He found it interesting and started plugging numbers in here and there to see what would happen. Yes, he learned quite a bit about the program that day, while messing up a database critical to the business. Restoring the file from a backup solved the problem.

"Arnold," my friend said, "What were you doing in there?"

"Well," he said, "I wanted to check the status of an account, and things just kept getting more interesting. I thought I could simply abandon the file and I could leave it as I found it."

"So could you?"

"Apparently not. Nobody ever told me that databases save automatically."

"If you're waiting for people to 'tell you things,' you're going to have a really hard time in business. If you know what you're doing, do it. If you don't, then don't. But you also need to stick to your job. You've got plenty of things to worry about without getting into other people's territory. They won't take to it kindly."

I'm sure my friend delivered another few lessons related to the incident. And our young hero? He didn't last long at this job or the next two, but then suddenly the light bulb went on and he's a valued—and valuable—manager at a manufacturing company.

Assign a Mentor

The scheduled commonsense review sessions may not be as effective being led by the boss as they would if they were led by a mentor. A mentor is a professional role model who takes a personal interest in the employee. They might trade e-mails each day, have lunch once a week, or just chat sporadically throughout the year. Seasoned professionals offer guidance to aspiring careerists. Female executives help other women crack the glass ceiling. Wise alumni take uncertain young graduates under their wing. And a carefully chosen mentor can help your employees, over time, get a good grasp on their common sense.

Finding effective mentors is, admittedly, tough. Not only must the mentors possess solid common sense themselves, but they must be able to converse comfortably with the trainees. It's harder to play matchmaker for a potential marriage, but not a whole lot harder. Consider these tips for being a successful, mentoring yenta:

- Don't be afraid to approach someone to become a mentor. Almost everyone, especially at a senior level, understands the importance of mentoring, which means you may find that the more successful people are, the more receptive they will be to your inquiry. Most successful people are genuinely interested in helping others succeed.

- Understand that, although there are advantages to having a mentor with a background similar to the employee, you may find it more effective to select someone from a different department or one with a dissimilar personality style. For instance, if your employee's personality is outgoing, perhaps select a mentor who is reserved. If the employee is from marketing, match him with an accountant. The goal is to put employees with mentors who personally possess a high level of common sense and who have the ability to talk employees through different scenarios, providing their own slant on the issues.

- Stick to business. There is a natural urge to allow business advice to evolve into personal guidance. You are not seeking a therapist-type relationship. A mentor serves a specific business purpose; don't let the borders get fuzzy.

- Choose a member of the same sex; there are too many opportunities for misunderstandings, otherwise. Sometimes the problems become worse than misunderstandings. You don't want to ruin a great mentorship opportunity by creating a crisis.

- Don't arrange a mentor relationship with a person's supervisor or anyone in the employee's chain of command. There are too many opportunities for conflict and confusion about roles. ("Did you just tell me that as my boss or as my mentor?")

- Realize that the mentor doesn't have to be older, but this is usually best. Don't get too outside the box on this one.

Assigning a mentor to tutor employees' common sense is not overkill. A relationship must exist in which employees are comfortable sharing the details of their thought processes and even admit to some embarrassing decisions. These types of conversations are difficult to have with your boss. Employees are more apt to be defensive if their mentor is in their chain of command. Conversation is much more open and honest when held with an older, wiser mentor.

Note Mentors—professional role models—can help newer or less-experienced employees develop or improve their common sense.

Play Games

Why work at something when you can simply accomplish it through play-time? OK, perhaps we cannot master the skill of common sense entirely through playing games, but we can make some serious progress.

There are some fun activities that teach logic, judgment, and sensible behavior—in other words, common sense. One of the best ways to mix your education with fun is to take the next plane to Vegas. Some of these games, particularly poker and blackjack, require the development of strong analytical skills. Yes, on any individual hand luck does play a role, but this luck cancels itself out in the long run. What survives, and determines whether you are a good player, depends on the development of your analytical skills. Using poker to teach/learn common sense is a foolproof way to write off a trip to Vegas as a legitimate business expense on your tax returns. (Note: You should verify this with your accountant, who may have different advice.)

A milder and more domestically friendly way to play your way to common sense can be found in common board games such as chess, checkers, and backgammon. (Ever notice when a movie wants to show a character with down-home common sense, he's framed behind a checkerboard?) I agree that, because of the dice rolls, backgammon does have an element of luck, but it, again, evens out over time. All these games have the following in common: to get better, you must learn how to think and analyze. And this builds common sense.

But perhaps the best game for developing your common sense (and one that is considerably less expensive that poker) is to grab a book full of Sudoku puzzles. Sudoku requires pure logic and the puzzles are presented with an increasing skill level, so you can begin with simple, easily solved puzzles, then build your logic skills.

Here's how the puzzle works: You fill a nine-by-nine grid with digits one through nine so that each column, each row, and each of the nine three-by-three subgrids that compose the grid contain all the digits. There are some additional constraints. For example, the same integer may not appear twice in the same row, column, or in any of the nine three-by-three subregions of the grid.

Sudoku puzzles require no luck whatsoever. In fact, to solve a puzzle successfully, you must learn the several methods that can be used for discovering the one—and only one—possible entry for each spot. These methods require you to develop logic and analytical abilities. Furthermore, these abilities improve, and the number of methods for solving puzzles increases as the puzzles become more difficult.

Group Training

Make commonsense development a part of every group meeting. For instance, take 15 minutes during each meeting to brainstorm a situation or a problem. Get a healthy brainstorming discussion going during which everyone tries to suggest ways a situation could be handled reasonably. Here are some scenarios you could toss out:

- A fast-food restaurant chain wants to add a new product to its menu. Discuss the steps in the process, from product conception through rollout.

- The president has announced a national goal, before this decade is out, of landing a woman on Mars and returning her safely to Earth. What are the steps needed to accomplish this goal? What different departments will be needed to plan and execute this project?

- You must choose between two candidates for a position. One of them is animal dumb (and I'm not talking about a border collie or a dolphin) but has amazing people skills. The other is just the opposite—brilliant but obnoxious. Which do you select?

- Should laws be changed to allow individuals to sell one of their kidneys to patients needing a transplant?

- You are all members of a jury. The defendant is accused of intent to distribute narcotics. He was caught with 40 Xanax capsules and $15,000 in cash, in 20s and 10s. What might be reasons the person is guilty or not guilty? What is your verdict?

- Has Earth ever been visited by beings from another planet? What is the evidence for or against?

- Suppose you were to host our own version of the Academy Awards celebrating your employees. You want to recognize great achievement in a litany of varying skills and accomplishments. What awards should be presented?

Pick topics in which your employees have no technical knowledge whatsoever. For instance, if you are operating a restaurant chain, don't brainstorm the fast-food new-product scenario; instead, choose the mission to Mars. The trick is to have employees base their discussions completely on logic and common sense.

Of course, you could use this brainstorming exercise to ponder grand visions within your organization. During the 1980s I served as a vice president (VP) of the world's smallest conglomerate. We had ownership of a humble business buffet that included hotels, dinner theaters, coffee shops, (those were my territories), and several high-profile magazines. Sound impressive? Not really. We had revenue of about $4 million and profits 1 year of $11,000—not exactly a powerhouse organization.

During a quarterly retreat of the company's officers, we had several urgent items on the agenda. We discussed how to slash payroll, how to generate more sales in each division, and how to get our company cars out of the parking garage because the company was unable to pay that month's bill to the office building.

After a spirited discussion of these items, our president began a new topic. "My sources tell me that Opryland will soon be for sale. Let's talk a bit on how we can buy them." For those of you who don't follow Nashville business, let me tell you a bit about Opryland. This complex features a 2,000-room hotel and a large theme park, and it houses the Grand Ole Opry, among its several entertainment businesses. Annual revenues were north of half a billion dollars. All the VPs looked at each other when this announcement was made, thinking the same thing: *Our leader is a nutcase.*

But, he led us through the discussion using terms like *leverage* and *synergy* and such; soon, we all began contributing ideas. It became an exciting discussion and I must admit we all learned a tremendous amount about acquiring new companies.

No, we did not acquire Opryland, but that really wasn't the purpose of the exercise. The CEO wanted us to expand our vision and learn how to work together as a powerful team.[2] And, although we didn't purchase this entertainment juggernaut, what we learned that day did lead to us buying (in highly creative deals) another magazine as well as a small chain of restaurants.

Besides being fun and a great way for your team to learn to work together, this exercise exposes your employees to positive examples of logic and common sense. They'll learn from each other.

Common sense   Opportunities can drop in your lap, if you put your lap where opportunities tend to drop.

---

[2] We learned that, with proper teamwork and a fluid exchange of ideas, one plus one can equal five.

Have a Film Festival

You can take 2 years of your life and invest $50,000 and get an MBA. Or, you can pop a bag of popcorn in the microwave, pour yourself a tall glass of Coke Zero, and watch a great movie that teaches you some solid commonsense values.

Really. You would be surprised at the depth of common sense that can be acquired while being entertained. So use this painless method for teaching your employees about common sense. Here are some great movies tailor-made for teaching common sense. Assign your mentees one a week and follow it up with a great discussion over coffee. If they look for the message, they'll gain an MBA level in common sense.

Forrest Gump: When you strip away all the intellectual perspectives and allow your thoughts to be guided by the most basic facts, great wisdom can accidently pop up. Isn't it ironic that you can learn common sense from someone the rest of the world has labeled as an idiot?

> *Quote:* "You have to do the best with what God gave you."

Babe: Babe, a pig, teaches us amazing people skills (animal skills?), such as we should manage with influence rather than dominance. Go ahead; if a pig can do it, so can you. (Further irony: You are now learning common sense from livestock.)

> *Quote:* "I asked them and they did it. I just asked them nicely."

Pay It Forward: One person can make a difference. Forget about keeping score and paying back those that have done you a favor. Instead look for ways to help strangers unexpectedly.

> *Quote:* "I think some people are too scared or something. I guess it's hard for people who are so used to things the way they are—even if they're bad—to change."

Big Fish: A dying man is trying to reconcile with his son, who is exhausted from hearing his father's improbable yarns. But the reality is that, although the stories are exaggerations, they are based on fact. What may look like a wild dream to you just might be solid reality to someone else.

> *Quote:* "A man tells his stories so many times that he becomes the stories. They live on after him, and in that way he becomes immortal."

The Pursuit of Happyness: A homeless man takes care of his son, while triumphing in an internship with a brokerage company. You don't have to be a genius to succeed. Just show determination, self-belief, and perseverance. The protagonist fights crises and obstacles most of us couldn't even imagine, but he never gives up.

Quote: "It was right then that I started thinking about Thomas Jefferson on the Declaration of Independence and the part about our right to life, liberty, and the pursuit of happiness. And I remember thinking how did he know to put the pursuit part in there?"

Beauty and the Beast: A beautiful young woman learns to love a hideous monster. Judge people by the character they demonstrate rather than their first impression.

Quote: "We don't like what we don't understand. In fact, it scares us, and this monster is mysterious at least."

Yes Man!: How many times do you say no in life? Do you shut out opportunities without even realizing it? Jim Carey commits to saying yes to everything. Initially, this gets him into big trouble, but he eventually sees that there are a lot of surprising opportunities waiting if you are just open to them.

Quote: "What I have to share is huge—and I want to share it with you."

Braveheart: This biography of Scottish revolutionary William Wallace captures his amazing ability to lead his ragtag army. Watch how a leader inspires.

Quote: "There's a difference between us. You think the people of this country exist to provide you with position. I think your position exists to provide those people with freedom. And I've got to make sure that they have it."

The Godfather: Three hours of commonsense knowledge—proof that we can learn great ideals even from people with alien values.

Quote: "Someday, and that day may never come, I will call upon you to do a service for me. But until that day, consider this justice a gift on my daughter's wedding day."

The Ox-Bow Incident: A posse in the Old West hangs some horse thieves. Or at least they think they are horse thieves. Oops. A rush to judgment can yield horrific decisions.

Quote: "There's truth in lies too, if you can get enough of them."

Shawshank Redemption: A man is given a hopeless life sentence for a crime he did not commit. Despite his apparent desperation, he develops a long-term plan to reclaim his freedom. (And changes many lives in the process.) Your hope and outlook shapes your life, regardless of where you may be.

Quote: "Get busy living or get busy dying."

Singin' in the Rain: You can find pure joy in some of the most mundane things—such as rain.

> *Quote:* "What's the first thing an actor learns? 'The show must go on!' Come rain, come shine, come snow, come sleet, the show *must* go on!!"

Dr. Strangelove: A movie that spoofs common sense—or the total lack of it.

> *Quote:* "Gentlemen, you can't fight in here! This is the War Room!"

Groundhog Day: A day in a life repeats dozens of times. Disaster results as long as Bill Murray tries to control people and events. His life becomes fulfilling, however, when he decides simply to improve himself and unselfishly help others.

> *Quote:* "Well, what if there is no tomorrow? There wasn't one today."

A Face in the Crowd: Andy Griffith's first movie was certainly no comedy. This dark look at a young highwayman who becomes a radio and TV cult superstar shows what happens when some people get a hold of tremendous influence and power. Hypocrisy will catch up with you eventually.

> *Quote:* "I'll say one thing for him; he's got the courage of his ignorance."

Click: A workaholic architect finds a universal remote that allows him to fast-forward through the mundane parts of his life. We see how it is those routine times in life that add up to some of the most meaningful experiences.

> *Quote:* "He's always chasing the pot of gold, but when he gets there, at the end of the day, it's just corn flakes."

Of Mice and Men: George and Lennie wander the country, dreaming of a better life for themselves. Then, just as their dream is within their grasp, it is cruelly yanked away. Dreams don't always happen, even when you try to do everything right.

> *Quote:* "[A] guy don't need no sense to be a nice fella."

It's a Wonderful Life: Put your problems in perspective. George Bailey gets his wish and sees what the world would have been like if he had never been born. He learns that, although he thought his life was insignificant, the reality is he touched so many others in wonderful ways.

Quote: "A toast to my big brother, George: The richest man in town!"

The Elephant Man: Don't judge a book by its cover. 'Nuff said.

Quote: "I am not an elephant! I am not an animal! I am a human being! I am a man!"

E.T. the Extra-Terrestrial: A family is visited by an awkward but wise alien. The family learns that love comes in all shapes and sizes, and can be found in the most unconventional places.

Quote: "You could be happy here, I could take care of you. I wouldn't let anybody hurt you. We could grow up together, E.T."

A League of Their Own: This comedy/drama charts the adventures of the Rockford Peaches, a part of the All-American Girls Baseball League, which replaced Major League Baseball when the men were sent to fight World War II. All doubts about women's abilities and equality should have come to an end during World War II, when women ran this country while the men were fighting the war.

Quote: "Well I was just wonderin' why you would throw home when we got a two-run lead. You let the tying run get on second base and we lost the lead because of you. Start using your head. That's the lump that's three feet above your ass . . . . Are you crying? Are you crying? ARE YOU *CRYING*? There's no crying! THERE'S NO CRYING IN BASEBALL!"

Argo: The semitrue story about the rescue of American diplomats during the Iran hostage crisis of 1980. Nothing beats a well-crafted plan executed by dedicated people. With a little bit of luck.

Quote: "This is the best bad plan we have, sir."

Miracle on 34th Street: A kindly old man thinks he is Kris Kringle. A lawyer goes to court to prove Kris really is the one, the only, Santa Claus. At least once in your life, go ahead and fight for a hopeless cause.

Quote: "Faith is believing when common sense tells you not to."

Red Dawn: The United States is invaded by the entire Soviet army and ten really cool teenagers from small-town Michigan drive them off. Seriously. This movie is packed full of nonsense and gaps in logic. Watch it with pen and paper; see how complete of a list you can make of all the common nonsense. Sometimes the best way to learn what to do is to study what not to do. And the quote below is the dumbest line in the history of the movies.

Quote: "Things are different now."

Beau Geste: A movie all about mixed morality, family, crime, war, and decency.

> *Quote:* "Wait a minute. I don't know much about mutinies, but I do know it isn't good form to plan them at the top of your voice."

The Grapes of Wrath: The most desperate class deals with the lowest time in America's economy. With dignity.

> *Quote:* "Rich fellas come up an' they die, an' their kids ain't no good an' they die out. But we keep a-comin'. We're the people that live. They can't wipe us out; they can't lick us. We'll go on forever, Pa, 'cause we're the people."

Apollo 13: Their spaceship is on the way to a glorious moon landing when there is an explosion, imperiling the astronauts' lives and hopes for returning to Earth. Think your job has challenges?

> *Quote:* "Failure is not an option."

Mr. Smith Goes to Washington: An honest man is elected to the U.S. Senate, where his naiveté soon clashes with Washington corruption. Truth will eventually win out if good men refuse to be beaten.

> *Quote:* "I guess this is just another lost cause, Mr. Paine. All you people don't know about lost causes. Mr. Paine does. He said once they were the only causes worth fighting for. And he fought for them once, for the only reason any man ever fights for them; because of just one plain simple rule: 'Love thy neighbor.' ... And you know that you fight for the lost causes harder than for any other. Yes, you even die for them."

On the Waterfront: It can be a thin line between being a tragic failure and being "a contender."

> *Quote:* "You don't understand. I coulda had class. I coulda been a contender. I coulda been somebody, instead of a bum, which is what I am, let's face it."

Up: This heartwarming animation follows the journey of an old man pursuing the adventure he dreamed about since he was a small boy. You are never too old to live your dreams. And sometimes those dreams come with some wonderful surprises.

> *Quote:* "Adventure is out there!"

Citizen Kane: The entire movie is spent searching for the meaning of Kane's last word: *rosebud.* Kane himself once said, "I don't think there's one word that can describe a man's life." Yet, ironically, "rosebud" does a pretty good job of doing so.

> *Quote:* "I always gagged on the silver spoon."

Field of Dreams: A movie about baseball; therefore, it's a movie about life. That in itself makes it worth watching.

> *Quote:* "Heaven? No. It's Iowa."

Saving Private Ryan: Courage is not the absence of fear; it is doing the right thing regardless of that fear.

> *Quote:* "Earn this."

Finding Nemo: A fish gets lost in the ocean and struggles mightily to survive while his father searches for him. He endures with a lot of help from new friends. Risk everything for family and friends. It's worth it.

> *Quote:* "I am a nice shark, not a mindless eating machine. If I am to change this image, I must first change myself. Fish are friends, not food."

Million Dollar Baby: Even if the personalities and styles are polar opposites, people can team together successfully if they share a passion. (And if you really love someone, you will kill her if she asks you to.)

> *Quote:* "Anybody can lose one fight. Anybody can lose once. You'll come back from this; you'll be champion of the world."

All the President's Men: Dedicated, thorough professionals can defeat even the most powerful if they are fighting for the truth.

> *Quote:* "If you're gonna do it, do it right. If you're gonna hype it, hype it with the facts. I don't mind what you did. I mind the way you did it."

Schindler's List: A German businessman risks everything to save Jews from Nazi extinction. One man—even a terribly flawed one—can make a difference.

> *Quote:* "The list is life."

Toy Story: A friend in need is a friend indeed. We can achieve great things if we learn to work with others, regardless of their rather sizable flaws and limitations.

> *Quote:* "This isn't flying, this is falling with style!"

The Third Man: Sometimes, we have to learn the hard way that not everyone shares our ideals.

Quote: "In Italy, for 30 years under the Borgias, they had warfare, terror, murder, and bloodshed, but they produced Michelangelo, Leonardo da Vinci, and the Renaissance. In Switzerland, they had brotherly love. They had 500 years of democracy and peace, and what did that produce? The cuckoo clock."

Fiddler on the Roof: Consistently act on your principles, but don't be afraid to reexamine those actions with what you have learned and experienced in life.

Quote: "So would it disrupt some great cosmic plan if I had a small fortune?"

Charlie Chaplin's City Lights: My all-time favorite movie follows the Little Tramp as he stumbles into a plan to save his love's eyesight. Even those perceived as the least among us can change lives in wonderful ways.

Quote: " . . . "[3]

Rudy: You can't get enough messages about fighting the good fight. The last thing Rudy looks like is a football player, but he has the heart of a Super Bowl Most Valuable Player.

Quote: "I rode the bench for two years. Thought I wasn't being played because of my color, I got filled up with a lotta attitude. So I quit. Still not a week goes by I don't regret it. And I guarantee a week won't go by in your life you won't regret walking out, letting them get the best of ya."

Patton: This accurate biography of the great World War II general shows the complexity of his personality. Great men often possess great flaws.

Quote: "I thought I would stand here like this so you could see if I was really as big a son of a bitch as you think I am."

Bruce Almighty: We will question God many times in our life, but this movie helps us understand that He has a pretty tough job. Sometimes, what is so obvious just isn't.

Quote: "Parting your soup is not a miracle, Bruce; it's a magic trick. A single mom who's working two jobs and still finds time to take her son to soccer practice—that's a miracle. People want me to do everything for them. What they don't realize is 'they' have the power. You want to see a miracle, son? Be the miracle."

---

[3]*City Lights* is a silent movie.

Mister Roberts: A World War II supply ship deals with an idiot for a captain. Sometimes, the right thing to do is rebel against authority using whatever tools available.

> *Quote:* "Captain, it is I, Ensign Pulver, and I just threw your stinkin' palm tree overboard! Now what's all this crud about no movie tonight?"

Lincoln: Daniel Day Lewis blesses us with what may be the best acting performance in the history of filmmaking. Because of his incredible rendition, we get to see a man who displays pure genius that is completely derived from common sense. Amazing.

> *Quote:* "Things which are equal to the same things are equal to each other. In his book, Euclid says this is self-evident. You see there it is even in that 2,000-year-old book of mechanical law it is the self-evident truth that things which are equal to the same things are equal to each other."

Marty: We sometimes let casual remarks from others keep us from exploring opportunities that could change our lives for the better. Ignore the labels others put on you.

> *Quote:* "You don't like her. My mother don't like her. She's a dog. And I'm a fat, ugly man. Well, all I know is, I had a good time last night. I'm gonna have a good time tonight. If we have enough good times together, I'm gonna get down on my knees. I'm gonna beg that girl to marry me. You don't like her? That's too bad."

The Blind Side: *Family* has a lot of definitions. And one can be created even if some of its members come from a different place or DNA.

> *Quote:* "You threaten my son, you threaten me."

Slumdog Millionaire: This is a celebratory film that shows a person's ability to reject the path laid out for him and the ability to take his destiny into his own hands.

> *Quote:* "Shut up! The man with the Colt 45 says shut up!"

Elf: You can find good wherever you find yourself.

> *Quote:* "I just like to smile. Smiling's my favorite."

A Christmas Story: A young boy prepares for Christmas, plotting ways to receive his coveted BB gun. Never stop going after what you really want.

> *Quote:* "Over the years, I got to be quite a connoisseur of soap. My personal preference was for Lux, but I found Palmolive had a nice, piquant after-dinner flavor—heady, but with just a touch of mellow smoothness. Life Buoy, on the other hand . . . ."

Nashville: No profound message here. I've included it because about 20% was filmed in a dinner theatre I once owned.

> *Quote:* "Y'all take it easy now. This isn't Dallas; it's Nashville! They can't do this to us here in Nashville! Let's show them what we're made of. Come on everybody, sing!"

Twelve Angry Men: Sometimes the majority simply means that all the fools are on the same side.

> *Quote:* I don't care whether I'm alone or not! It's my right.

Amadeus: True geniuses rarely take their own work seriously, because it comes so easily for them. This is why great athletes and scholars make lousy coaches and teachers.

> *Quote:* "It's unbelievable! The director has actually torn up a huge section of my music. They say I have to rewrite the opera. But it's perfect as it is! I can't rewrite what's perfect!"

The Wizard of Oz: Quit waiting for someone to wave a magic wand. Instead, gather a (somewhat flawed) team around you, attack your problem head on, and take your destiny into your own hands. (Also, what you perceive as a weakness may actually be your strength.)

> *Quote:* "But some people without brains do an awful lot of talking. Don't they?"

▓ **Common sense**   Cream always rises to the top. Then again, so does grease.

Other Lessons Learned from Films

You can learn many life lessons from the movies, even beyond the basics of common sense. Here are a few of the important things you can learn about society, relationships, and even history if you pay close attention to the movies you watch.

- All grocery bags contain a stick of French bread.

- A man shows no pain while having the living crap beat out of him but winces when a beautiful woman cleans his wounds.

- Medieval peasants had perfect teeth.

- All single women own a cat and lip-sync Motown songs into a hairbrush they pretend is a microphone.

- Bad guys can't shoot straight.

- Fathers are so wrapped up in their careers they always forget their son's eighth birthday.

- Parking? No problem. It is always possible to park directly outside the building you are visiting.

- If it is nighttime, it will be raining.

- Detectives can only solve a case after they have been suspended.

- And during their suspension notification, the lieutenant sternly lectures, "You are your own worst enemy!"

- All phone numbers start with 555.

- Ancient Romans had British accents.

Betcha you can't learn this at Harvard.

Summary

There is a debate whether common sense is something you are born with or something you can learn. I obviously believe that it can be learned. Most of this learning comes by osmosis; we absorb the thought processes of those we are close to.

This process begins with our parents. A dozen plus years of observing their processes, both good and bad, constitutes a lot of learning. (And, because this information is absorbed mainly during our early years, we reflect our parents' level of common sense—thus the reason many believe the trait is inherited.) Later, we learn from our friends and business associates, as well as the books we read and, yes, the movies we watch.

Common sense is most definitely a learned experience. It's not conventional learning, like math or science; rather, it is the sum of what we absorb. You can't go to school to get this learning, but it can be acquired if you seek it out.

Besides, the cinema is a heck of a lot more fun than the lecture hall.

Understanding People

The Cornerstone of Common Sense

Many years ago, I had a watershed moment in the evolution of my own personal common sense. One morning, just a few weeks before Christmas, my secretary[1] stuck her head in my office and announced, "I want your permission to take next Tuesday off as a personal day."

"Sure," I replied without looking up from my paperwork. "That will be fine."

Janet continued. "I have already finished all the reports that will be due and I have talked to Shelby. She will cover anything you need that might pop up that day."

"Okay. Fine, thanks." I responded. Not only did I not look up, but I was able to actually sign my name to three expense reports while grunting my approval to her.

Janet continued. "I have lots of personal leave days accumulated, so there will be no problem with the payroll."

At this point, I truly was getting a bit restless, tiring of being told all this unnecessary information. "OK," I grunted.

---

[1] You can tell this occurred in the 1980s, because it was still politically correct to refer to your administrative assistant as your *secretary*.

Janet continued. "What I am going to do is to try to get a head start on my Christmas shopping. There is a big sale at Macy's and I think I will get a lot done there."

"Janet, okay, I get it," I barked. Now I was looking directly into her eyes, making no secret that I was a bit exasperated for all the unnecessary details. "Enjoy your day off. But for today, do you have that rough draft of my monthly report?"

Janet's eyes almost teared up as she left my office saying, "I'll get that for you right away." Eavesdropping on her, I heard Janet tell Shelby in an irritated voice, "Ken hasn't got the common sense to even listen when I try to explain something important to him."

That statement shocked me. Here I was with a 154 IQ, rather solid educational credentials, and a list of training programs longer than the Italian peninsula, yet I was being accused of not having any common sense whatsoever.

After a lot of introspective analysis, I finally figured out what had happened that day. Janet and I possessed complete and opposite personality types. Janet came from a group that needs to explain details and to be listened to. I, on the other hand, am in a group that likes information short, direct, and to the point. No wasted words. Understand that I had worked with Janet for several years and had complete and total confidence in her. If she said she was taking care of something or that she needed something, or that she thought something, I did not need any further detail. In this case, Janet said she was going to take Tuesday off. I needed no further explanation. Here was the basis of our conflict: I thought I was displaying trust in my reaction; Janet thought I was uncaring. Could we both be right?[2]

Those lacking good common sense believe all people are basically the same, should be dealt with in the same manner, and expect people's behavior to be identical in similar situations. Those with good common sense understand people have different needs and should be dealt with differently.

Let me explain. Have you ever met someone and could immediately relate to him, feeling you had known him your whole life? On the other hand, have there been people in your life that, no matter how hard you try, you just can't seem to make a connection? These interactions happen when

---

[2] Taking an odd perspective, I told myself that my response was actually a compliment to her.

varying personality types meet. The people you immediately click with are probably your same type, whereas the ones you cannot build a rapport with are from one of the other personality groups.

This ability to relate successfully to different types of people can be learned. Let me introduce one way in which I have combined several of the more successful personality-style identification systems. Mastering the ability to relate with people will help you understand your coworkers and communicate more effectively with them, regardless of how similar or opposite they may be to your own style.

Tip You can learn to interact constructively with many different personality types. It's well worth the effort and can take you far in your career.

First, a little background. Beginning with Socrates, social observers have known that people generally fall into one of four distinct personality types. Early philosophers named these types phlegmatic, sanguine, choleric, and melancholic. (Early philosophers were poor marketers.) Contemporary systems identify these same types using more palatable terms such as fire, air, earth, and water; red, yellow, blue, and white; DiSC (dominant, influence, steady, and conscientious; or NT, SP, NF, and SJ (in the Keirsey scheme). All of these type names have a good basis for describing their personalities, but are a bit confusing to keep straight by label alone. To make this easier, we will use some descriptors and play off the fact that *birds of a feather flock together*. We will call our four personality types the Peacock, the Owl, the Dove, and the Eagle.[3]

Common sense "Never claim as a right what you can ask as a favor." —*John Churton Collin*

Identifying the Bird

In a moment, we will go into some detail about each style, but first let me show you a quick way to determine each person's category. We can do this by answering two questions:

---

[3]My initial system referred to them as Creators, Connectors, Commanders, and Cogetators in a rather confusing desire to have them all begin with the same letter.

1. Is the person direct or indirect in their communication? When an indirect people are hungry and want to eat lunch, they will ask, "Are you hungry? Would you like to go get something to eat? You don't want to go to Applebee's do, you?" Whereas direct people in the same situation will say, "I'm hungry. Let's eat lunch. How about Applebee's?"

2. Is the person open or private in telling about themselves? This question deals with how willing people are to let you get to know them. There are some people who, within minutes of your meeting them, will lay out their life story. They find it easy to express their feelings and let you know what those feelings are. Others prefer to play it close to the vest and keep their thoughts to themselves. Knowing what's really on their mind requires a team of horses tugging mightily at their brainstem.

The answers to these two questions tell you which category of bird you are dealing with. Here's how it breaks down:

- **Dove:** Indirect and open
- **Peacock:** Direct and open
- **Owl:** Indirect and private
- **Eagle:** Direct and private

Now that we have categorized the four styles, let's learn a bit about the personalities of each of these birds.

Note   People usually fall in two of the four categories: indirect or direct, and open or private. How these categories intersect reveals much about the people you deal with on a daily basis.

The Creative Peacock

Peacocks are direct in communication and open in expressing feelings. They are the people who come up with lots of big ideas and sell those ideas enthusiastically. Peacocks don't just express an opinion; they also have a great story to illustrate their point.

People are attracted to Peacocks. They appear genuine, approachable, and communicate brilliantly. However, Peacocks can also be disappointing to some of the very people they attract. This is because Peacocks bite off more than they can chew and rarely finish any project themselves. They are visionaries, for sure, but their participation often stops with the vision. Peacocks appear to have many friends, but rarely are those friends very close. Most could be referred to more accurately as social acquaintances.

Peacocks do not attempt to control others, and they are just as passionate about not being controlled. They will, in fact, shun the company of people they perceive are trying to run their lives, primarily because they have no interest in running the lives of others. (You could consider Peacocks as "social libertarians.") This complete resistance to control often makes Peacocks difficult—even exasperating—to manage.

Because of their need for excitement and creativity, Peacocks are often led to occupations such as entertainer, artist, actor, firefighter, gambler, tour guide, professional wrestler, activist, negotiator, advertising executive, or salesperson.

Peacocks are exciting to know, fun to be around, and bring important contributions to the work team. They generate high-quality and high-quantity ideas. They are enthusiastic and handle emergencies well. Their weaknesses are just a blatant, however. Working with Peacocks can be frustrating because they rarely follow through on their dynamic ideas. They see themselves as big-picture people and assume the details take care of themselves. They don't, of course—a fact Peacocks don't realize because they are too busy moving on to the next great idea.

When angry, Peacocks may resort to sarcasm. They know where each person's soft spot is and they go right for the jugular, if necessary. If they feel they are being ignored, Peacocks do things to call attention to themselves. In extreme cases, they may even act in a bizarre manner.

There are many examples of Peacocks in the movies and the history books. Consider these famous Peacocks: Jay Leno, Conon O'Brien, David Letterman, Babe Ruth, the Wizard in *The Wizard of Oz*, and our most recent three presidents: Bill Clinton, George W. Bush, and Barack Obama.

You can spot a Peacock easily by noticing some stereotypical (and exaggerated) mannerisms. For instance, typical Peacocks drive a shiny red sports car, wear all the latest fashions, and are in sync with all the current fads. The office of a Peacock may be a bit disheveled or unorganized, with lots of knick-knacks laying around—each with a really great story attached.[4]

Common sense   "The audience is always right." —*Woody Allen*

---

[4]For those of you wanting to reconcile two pop psychology theories, you usually find the Peacock is the youngest child in birth order.

The Wise Owl

Owls are indirect in their communication and keep their thoughts private. Owls are very good with information and are outstanding planners. They are rational and (often) humor-challenged.

Because they are so introspective, Owls rarely try to control others, but often find themselves being controlled by others. Owls do not like to show emotion and consider doing so a weakness. When under pressure, Owls may frown, clam up, fold their arms across their chest, and say, "If you don't care to hear my thoughts, I'll just keep them to myself."

An Owl's strengths radiate competence. They are fair, and great with details and data. They brief subordinates thoroughly on their specific roles, duties, and performance benchmarks. No detail escapes an Owl; procedures are well known and invariably enforced. Unfortunately, their process focus may cause them to get bogged down in details. Owls often cannot see the forest for the trees, which causes them to make tail-wagging-the-dog decisions. Owls can spend so much time planning for contingencies they never start anything. They often don't realize some decisions just do not warrant detailed study.

Owls love to work with details, procedures, and data, and are obsessed with *the process*. Accordingly, they are often drawn to careers involving these traits, such as bookkeeper, psychologist, scientist, novelist, mechanic, coroner, IRS agent, baseball umpire, bureaucrat, accountant, or engineer.

You have noticed that Owls are, in many ways, the opposite of Peacocks. Although Peacocks are great visionaries, Owls have trouble imagining new ideas. And although Owls are brilliant at detail and follow-through, Peacocks resist anything resembling bureaucracy. These differences can be the basis for great conflict. However, if each bird recognizes the other possesses traits he or she is deficient in, a great partnership can develop. These birds can do what they do best and rely on other to plug the holes in a project.

Examples of famous Owls include *Star Trek*'s Mr. Spock, *Star Wars*' Yoda, *The Godfather*'s Don Corleone, the Scarecrow in *The Wizard of Oz*, as well as presidents Woodrow Wilson, Herbert Hoover, and Jimmy Carter.

Stereotypical Owls are easy to identify. They never drive a fancy sports car; instead, they have a perfectly maintained, practical sedan, usually one that was rated a Best Buy by *Consumer Reports* magazine. Their office is neat and well organized, and may feature charts and graphs framed on the wall. On their desk is a formal family portrait, with each member dressed in their Sunday best.[5]

 Common sense The trouble with life in the fast lane is you get to the other end in an awful hurry.

The Team-Building Dove

Doves are indirect in communication but quite open about telling people their thoughts and feelings (unless they think their thoughts might upset the listener). We learn their entire life story within minutes of meeting them. The most important thing to realize about Doves is that they love to be surrounded by people and want to be friends with everyone. They carry a strong sense of tradition and have strict views on what is proper or improper, right or wrong. Although Doves are outwardly accepting, in reality they can be somewhat intolerant and judgmental. Despite their good nature, Doves quietly hold grudges, keep score, and find it hard to forgive.

Being indirect, they tend to make statements by asking (often rhetorical) questions. For instance, if Doves want to eat lunch, they ask, "Are you hungry?" If Doves want to visit a retail store, they'll ask, "Did you want to go to Walmart?"

Doves are, surprisingly, controlling of others and are often controlled by others. Their controlling personality comes from a sincere desire for good things to happen for others and their overwhelming need to be caretakers. Because they genuinely feel they know what is best, they attempt to influence others to act as the Dove feels is best for them. Because Doves are compliant and willingly self-sacrificing, they're often easily controlled themselves.

Doves make great friends and coworkers. They are loyal and dependable, timely and accurate. Doves love people and truly care about them as individuals. They are superb listeners and excellent people to bounce an idea off of. First and foremost, Doves are team builders.

---

[5]Owls pop up in various places in the birth order, but it is typical to see them as the second child in a four-sibling household.

Too good to be true? Well, kind of. Doves are more concerned with how things affect people than with accomplishing a goal. They can be overly sensitive, react poorly to criticism, and seek so much input that they are indecisive. Doves are quite resistant to change and see many issues as black or white; gray does not exist. Rather than solve problems, Doves often spend their time worrying about them.

When under pressure, Doves get very quiet and even sulk. They may purse their lips, but show no other outward signs of anger. Although it may appear initially as though Doves ignore injustices done to them, the real story is that they do not forget them. Doves collect these violations in a special place in their memory and explode one day. God help the person who added the final straw to the Dove's back.

How can you spot Doves? Whimsical indications include them serving as a Cub Scout Den leader even though they have no children. And they have a pet puppy that, curiously, has stayed a puppy for the past six years. Like the Owl, the Dove's office is neat and organized, but it also includes lots of pictures of friends and family (and Doves want to tell you about every one of their children, grandchildren, and cousins). They usually drive a larger vehicle (so they can fit all their friends). They chatter incessantly on the phone with friends while running errands, although they feel so very guilty about using a cell phone while driving.

Consider these famous Doves: Dorothy and the Tin Man from *The Wizard of Oz*, Gandhi, Mary Richards from *The Mary Tyler Moore Show*, and president George H.W. Bush.

Doves seek a career direction that appeals to their nurturing instincts. Such occupations include minister, teacher, social worker, nurse, counselor, caretaker, gardener, negotiator, and envoy.[6]

■ **Common sense**   "Do you want to make friends? Be friendly." —*Dale Carnegie*

The Bold Eagle

Eagles are direct in communication, even to the point of being cold and insensitive. They keep their personal feelings to themselves, and it is difficult to read their mood. (This makes Eagles solid poker players. In fact, an

---

[6]Being a natural peacemaker, most Doves are the middle child in the sibling birth order.

Eagle can wipe out a Peacock after just an hour of five-card draw.) Eagles insist on power and are action oriented. Although this results in getting a lot of things done, it often means people are trampled, and their mangled bodies are left in the Eagle's wake. Eagles have few friends but many business acquaintances with whom they have cultivated "mutually beneficial relationships."

Eagles are controllers, often to the point of being manipulative. Unlike Doves, who attempt to control people to get the best thing for the other person, Eagles control people for their own personal profit. Being in control is central to the Eagle psyche. Therefore, Eagles never allow themselves to be controlled and they react angrily to anyone's attempt to do so.

Eagles are take-charge leaders who get things done. Eagles take no excuses, are strongly goal oriented, grasp the big picture, and can cut through the clutter to get to the heart of an issue. These traits make Eagles powerful leaders, potentially.

These strengths, not surprisingly, also lead directly to their weaknesses. Eagles can be dogmatic and dictatorial. They like to make decisions alone—something they see as being decisive and a symbol of their competence. They rarely invite others to give them advice and they believe asking for help is a weakness. Although Eagles get things done, they often leave a scorched path in their wake. You don't want to anger Eagles. Their eyes will cut right through you as they verbally eviscerate you. (Okay, that was a bit overboard, but so is an Eagle.)

Eagles are drawn to careers in which they are in charge and make lots of decisions. Some obvious choices include military officers, chefs, pilots, football coaches, surgeons, police officers, and lawyers.

Examples of famous Eagles include General George Patton, Coach Vince Lombardi, the Cowardly Lion and the Wicked Witch from *The Wizard of Oz*, Hillary Clinton, England's Margaret Thatcher, and presidents Lyndon Johnson and Richard Nixon.

Whimsical indications you're with an Eagle include the following: they drive a black Hummer, smoke cigars, and have a pit bull for a pet. Their office features lots of mahogany furniture and their office door is generally kept closed. There is a large plaque on their desk that announces not only their name (including the middle initial), but also their rather impressive title.[7]

---

[7]Birth order? You guessed it. The Eagle is the first-born child.

A NOTE ABOUT THE STYLES

The four birds I've just listed represent *predominant* styles. There are exceptions. People rarely are one style; they exhibit traits from one of the other styles. For example, there are Peacocks who are excellent with details. (I, for instance, am a Peacock, but I love to analyze—a trait found more commonly in Owls.) You will find Eagles who are actually quite compassionate, as well as Doves who take charge from time to time. I've even known a couple of Owls who could tell a pretty good joke. Don't get hung up on finding all the exceptions and variances. Doing so would turn this into a tail-wagging-the-dog exercise. Just learn how to identify people by their primary style so you can understand quickly how to deal with them most effectively.

So What?

Right now you're probably thinking, *All this is quite interesting, but what do I do with this information?*

By understanding where people come from in their thinking and actions, you will be able to relate to them more effectively. Your communications will be smoother, clearer, and more successful. There is less chance for miscommunication—and misunderstanding. When people are able to communicate with you clearly and feel you understand them, they feel you are a sensible person with, well, good common sense. In fact, this ability to understand and relate to people might be the base on which common sense is built.

So let's take this whole concept further and see how we can use it in our relationships with others.

Tip Understanding personality types helps you put others at ease. When you and others are at ease, productive work gets done.

Enhance Relationships by Treating People Differently

So far in this book, I've angered Republicans, Democrats, Liberals, Conservatives, tree huggers, as well as coal miners. Now let me add a new group—my fellow Christians. Here goes: If you want to be able to relate to all types of people, it is important that you *do not* follow the Golden Rule. How is that? Look at what the Golden Rule states. *Do unto others as you would have others do unto you.* In other words, treat people exactly the way you want to be treated. This philosophy works only a fourth of the time simply because there are three personality styles other than the one you possess. If I may be so bold, the Bible should be edited to read: *Do unto others in a manner they wish to be done unto.*

Doves must be approached differently than Eagles. Peacocks cannot be talked to in the same manner as Owls. Doing so causes conflict and confusion, and makes it look like you have no common sense whatsoever. If you talk to an Owl as you would a Peacock, the Owl will be repulsed by your constant chattering and needless assertiveness. If you approach an Eagle as you would a Dove, the Eagle will think you are wimpy. Learn to approach people in the style they display to have the richest relationship with them.

Let's take this lesson in psychology and boil it down to one good application for business. Let's say you are proposing a project to two department heads—one is an Eagle and the other, an Owl. To the Eagle you should declare your bottom line in the first sentence of your memo, which should be followed by a bulleted-list explanation of your reasoning. The Eagle will probably approve your proposal after reading the very first line. However, if she does need more information, you have provided it in the list, and the Eagle will be comforted knowing more information is there if she really wants it.

The other department head may be an Owl, meaning it is just as important to him that he sees how you reached your decision than the decision itself. When writing to the Owl, write his memo opposite to the way you did for the Eagle. Begin by listing the problem, followed by several possible solutions. Include the reasons why you decided on your proposed course of action, followed by a concise statement of what that decision is. (And be sure to thank him for taking the time to read your memo.)

Note the tension you would create if you were to reverse the styles. If the Eagle received the second memo, she would think you're being tentative and wasting her time with a lot of unnecessary detail. However, the Owl might consider the Eagle's memo as being rash. He would fear you had failed to consider all reasonable options and merely jumped to a quick decision. He might even interpret your memo as you trying to put something past him.

Using Bird Styles to Build a Team

You can use this knowledge of the four personality styles as a common-sense method to build a team. To build a good, functioning team, you must have representatives from each of the birds. Before I explain why, let me show you what happens if you make the mistake many business people make, which is to surround yourself with people exactly like you. Let's look at the results that you get from having a team made up of only one style.

All Doves: Nothing will get done, but everyone will get along and know the names of each other's children. (Actually, even that might not happen, because they will all stop at the door and say, "After you." "No, please, you go first." And no one will enter the room.)

All Owls: This team will look like it is accomplishing a great deal. However, nothing will get done simply because the Owls will spend their time defining the process and setting up rules for operation.

All Peacocks. This would be a fun team to be a part of because you would hear all sorts of wonderful anecdotes. Little would be accomplished, however, because all their time would be spent with each Peacock trying to outdo the previous story.

All Eagles. Finally, something would get done. But only after one of the Eagles has killed the others and taken total control of the project.

OK. So this exercise is a satire, but not a huge exaggeration. When you gather a team in which everyone has all the same strengths and weaknesses, results will be incomplete and pretty darn frustrating.

So how should the team be assembled? By having representatives of each bird, you will be able to capture everyone's strengths and be able to compensate for the weaknesses. Imagine a team that includes a Peacock who shares a great vision along with creative solutions. Working with those ideas is an Owl, who designs the process for making these things happen as well as creates a workable schedule. Then you have the Dove, who encourages everyone to give their best and who ensures peaceful resolutions to all healthy conflict. And topping it off is an Eagle, who keeps the team focused on tasks and, most of all, makes sure the job gets done.

These dynamic results can be produced by a diverse team as long as one awareness exists. Each member must understand the strengths the others bring to the table and must respect that diversity. If there is shared respect, great things will happen. If there is no respect and understanding, chaos and conflict is inevitable.

▩ **Tip** When building a team, go out of your comfort zone and recruit people you know have different personalities than your own. It's not just desirable; it's essential.

In a 1995 interview, Steve Jobs told of his introduction to healthy conflict among a diverse team. When he was just a small boy—perhaps eight years old—he visited a family friend. This neighbor was an older man who loved to share wisdom with youngsters. He showed Jobs a crude machine in his garage. The gadget was a cylinder about the size of a coffee can with a pulley hooked up to a small motor. "Grab a couple of rocks from the yard," the man said. Jobs handed him two or three rather ugly rocks that were beside the porch. The man placed them in the cylinder along with sand and water. He then turned on the contraption, which proceeded to tumble the rocks, making a rather unpleasant, loud clanking noise. He then said, "Come back tomorrow, Steve, and let's see what we've got."

Jobs returned the next day. The old man unplugged the machine, opened the top of the cylinder, and removed the contents. Out came several beautiful, polished gems.

"That's where I learned all about effective teams," Jobs recalled. "You see, if you put talented people together and let them brainstorm a project, good things will happen. But those good things will only happen after a lot of whirling and banging and conflict. Successful teamwork can be noisy, but if they share their ideas and strengths, great things result."[8]

Summary

Understanding the nature of others is the key to successful communication. Learn to deal with people the way they want to be dealt with. This is not manipulation; it is showing courtesy and respect for the perspectives of others. Carry this understanding as you react to the words and actions of other people having different styles than yours. For instance

- Be patient when the Dove wants to explain every detail of her plans when she is asking for a day off

- Don't take it personally when your enthusiastic, "Good morning! How are you doing today!" is met with a terse "I'm fine" by an Owl.

- Don't be insulted if your Eagle coworker has no interest in sharing deep personal feelings with you.

- And don't roll your eyes when your sales manager has to tell you an amusing anecdote before giving you the data you requested. It's just his nature.

---

[8]*Steve Jobs: The Lost Interview,* 2012, Netflix.

Common sense is more than the decision-making process. Thoughts have no power if they are not passed along to others. Common sense has, as its cornerstone, the ability to relate to others and to transfer those thoughts in a manner others can best digest them. Getting to know these four birds will go a long way in helping you do this, and you will develop a reputation for having some impressive common sense along the way.

When Common Sense Fails

All this praise of common sense may be leading you to think of it as an intellectual cure-all. As critical as common sense is to a well-functioning intellect, let's be careful not to paint it as the all-inclusive trait. Common sense has its limitations and is ripe for misuse. In the words of ancient mapmakers, *Here there be dragons*.

The Perversion of Common Sense

Unfortunately, common sense is not a perfect tool. In fact, it can lead to horrid consequences. Consider the tragedy of Richard Jewell. Jewell was a rather mild-mannered young man, pudgy and overweight, who landed a dream job as a security guard at the 1996 Atlanta Olympics. Dream job? Yes, it was Jewell's dream to be a police officer. Although he had been rejected from the many forces to which he had applied, he just knew having a position with the Olympics would turbocharge his résumé.

One of Jewell's first assignments was to patrol the area of Olympic Park where, in the wee hours of July 27, 1996, fans and athletes alike were dancing to joyful music. Jewell was patrolling the celebration when he spotted something suspicious—an abandoned backpack. He reacted in an odd fashion. Somehow, assuming it could be a terrorist bomb, he loudly ordered everyone out of the area. Most thought he was overreacting, a power play by a rent-a-cop, but they complied nonetheless. Moments later, the package exploded, firing nails and shrapnel through the air.

Initially, the media lauded Jewell's good judgment. Although two people died because of the explosion, many more would have died if he hadn't taken action. But a few days later, a local paper reported that the FBI was investigating Richard Jewell for being the bomber! TV cameras descended on his home, making special note that he still lived with his mother. Reporters followed him wherever he went, thrusting microphones into his chunky face. Photographers captured the sad man with the deer-caught-in-the-headlights look in his eyes, and framed him with shots of his terrified mother. The theory that developed was that Jewell was a wannabe cop who had been a nobody all his life. Common sense proved that he had planted the bomb himself so he could be a hero for discovering it.[1] He probably assumed he would spend the rest of his days fielding offers from police departments and having his choice of beautiful southern girls. And it all made sense. Perfect sense. Common sense.

Here's the problem with this obvious conclusion: It was wrong. Richard Jewel did not plant the bomb.

Common sense clearly indicated that Richard Jewell was a pathetic young man who killed people. However, common sense was wrong. Richard Jewell was, indeed, a hero. His actions saved hundreds of lives and—I am not exaggerating here—probably saved the modern Olympic movement. But despite an unprecedented statement from the FBI, the confession of the real terrorist, and even a proclamation from the governor of Georgia, Richard Jewell was forever perceived by many as the redneck who had "gotten away with murder."

There was a similar case in which common sense destroyed a life. You are familiar with the horrid murder of JonBenet Ramsey on Christmas Eve in 1996. Common sense implied she was murdered by her own mother. Even the governor of Colorado issued a not-too-subtle statement declaring Patsy Ramsey guilty. The public grumbled because the police and prosecutors dragged their feet in making the obvious arrest. Then, with

---

[1] This is in keeping with the hero arsonist syndrome, a psychological condition that drives a person to set a house on fire so he can enjoy the acclaim he gets when he rushes in to save a child.

great fanfare, the police admitted that even though it was so very obvious Ramsey had murdered her daughter, they just didn't have enough evidence to convict.

In 2008, newly discovered DNA techniques *proved* Ramsey was innocent. The most hated woman in America was actually the victim of the cruelest claim that could ever be placed on a human being. Unfortunately, Ramsey never got to witness the reversal of her image. She died of cancer just a few months earlier.

One more. For more than 30 years Lindy Chamberlain was mocked as the lady who proclaimed, "A dingo ate my baby." Common sense showed her claim was preposterous. But the facts—and an Australian court—proved her story was true. However, instead of receiving deserved sympathy for this horrible event, Mrs. Chamberlain has been a comedic cliché for decades.

Each of these good people had to prove their innocence. It's not supposed to be that way. These three tragedies may indicate why our legal standard for conviction is "beyond a reasonable doubt," rather than a reliance on simple common sense.

Note When common sentiment is nearly unanimous in condemning a person's supposed actions, society has an obligation to ask, "But what if it's not true?"

The Frustration of Applying Commonsense Principles

Sometimes, common sense is not simply wrong, it can be frustratingly contradictory. Consider these timeless yet opposing expressions of common sense:

- Actions speak louder than words versus The pen is mightier than the sword.

- Look before you leap versus He who hesitates is lost.

- Many hands make light work versus Too many cooks spoil the broth.

- A silent man is a wise one versus A man without words is a man without thoughts.

- Beware of Greeks bearing gifts versus Don't look a gift horse in the mouth.

- Clothes make the man versus Don't judge a book by its cover.

- The squeaky wheel gets the grease versus The nail that sticks out gets hammered.

- Nothing ventured, nothing gained versus A bird in the hand is worth two in the bush.

- The best things in life are free versus You get what you pay for.

- The bigger, the better versus The best things come in small packages.

- Absence makes the heart grow fonder versus Out of sight, out of mind.

- What will be, will be versus Life is what you make it.

- Cross your bridges when you come to them versus Forewarned is forearmed.

- With age comes wisdom versus Out of the mouth of babes come wise sayings.

- The more the merrier versus Two's company; three's a crowd.

- Birds of a feather flock together versus Opposites attract.

And although Christians are admonished to take an eye for an eye, we are then told to turn the other cheek. Whew. Although we may be sincere in trying to institute common sense in our decision making, it becomes difficult when conventional wisdom often seems to argue with itself.

Common Sense Has Its Limits

Let's look at another compendium of common sense: common law. Common law is law established by summarizing decisions of the past and using these decisions as a basis for all future decisions. For instance, if a magistrate had seen 20 cases of a farmer stealing a dozen chickens from his neighbor and decided to fine the chicken thief six months in jail and fine of $100, then it becomes common law that the punishment for stealing 12 chickens is six months and a hundred bucks. Common law is established.

Common sense works the same way. Common sense is an established decision based on consistent decisions made in the past. Common law and common sense work quite well as long as circumstances don't change. But what happens to common law when chickens are replaced with more valuable alpacas or there are 500 animals involved instead of a dozen? The circumstances are altered and so the situation giving rise to common law are just not the same. And there is the rub.

Peter Drucker makes this point: "The greatest danger in times of turbulence is not the turbulence; it is to act with yesterday's logic."[2] Sadly, common sense often uses yesterday's logic to address today's new problems. When evaluating current problems, we can forget many of the factors that initially went in to our previous decision making, and even subconsciously exclude dynamics that existed when the previous logic was applied. More important, today's circumstances may be radically different from those that existed when we developed this common sense base.

This conundrum is seen readily in business when trying to predict the viability of a new product. Can common sense based on accumulated experience be helpful to decision makers forced to predict the future in complex situations? If all we need is basic common sense, why can't we predict the success of a strategy, a new disruptive technology, a product, or an advertisement? It is because these phenomena are too complex, involving so many variables that they can't fully mirror past experiences that led us to develop our common sense.

In the old days, soft drinks were sold in fast-food restaurants on a per-drink basis. In other words, you bought a drink and if you wanted more you had to purchase another drink. Because of this, restaurants sold drinks in multiple sizes, usually small, medium, and (very) large. In 1990, my company decided to test accessible fountains in one of my markets (Atlanta). We would save labor because now guests would get their own drink. But, guests could also go back to the fountain and get as many free refills as they wanted. Because of this, I assumed that it would be silly to continue offering three sizes of drinks. Common sense declared that because customers could get unlimited refills, they would only buy

---

[2] Peter F. Drucker, *Managing in Turbulent Times* (New York, NY: Harper Paperbacks, 1980).

the small drink and refill it multiple times. This was so obvious that I was about to change our selection to a single size. Fortunately, a wise marketing manager (this is not an oxymoron) thought it would first be a good idea just to see what would happen if we maintained the traditional three sizes. Reluctantly, I went against my usual sound commonsense skills and watched the results.

You guessed it, sales of the large drink size actually increased. This defied all common sense and to this day I cannot explain why.

Here is the bottom line in using common sense in business decisions: Common sense works when all things are constant and the environment is stable. Use your common sense, of course, but recognize that the situation may include new variables that must be part of your analysis.

If you get lost in the woods, it is good to have survival experience, but it is also nice to have a map.

Common sense "We use 10% of our brains. Imagine what we could accomplish if we used the other 60%." —*Ellen DeGeneres*

How to Win at *Jeopardy!*

Another problem with common sense is that we often only recognize decisions as common sense after we receive the correct answer. Here is a good example: In 1947, the War Department published a study called The American Soldier. A blue-ribbon collection of sociologists interviewed more than half a million soldiers about their experiences while serving in the Army during World War II. After the study was published, sociologist Paul Lazarsfeld wrote an analysis of the study, including the conclusion that, in the army, men from rural backgrounds fared better than men from cities.

The public's response was that this conclusion was rather obvious. Common sense would tell you that *of course* men from rural backgrounds did better than men from cities. After all, men from the country are used to sleeping on the ground and getting up before dawn. They're used to long hours of hard physical labor. The theoretical response to the report's conclusion was: Why did we need such a vast and expensive study to tell us what we could have figured out using our own common sense?

Lazarsfeld's response? "Good point, except that the results I told you were exactly the opposite of the results that the study actually found." In fact, the report concluded that city men did *better* than their rural counterparts.

Here is the point: If Lazarsfeld had reported the correct answer in the first place, *that* conclusion would have been perceived as obvious. Readers would have pulled together other factors, such as city men are used to working in large groups with a strict chain of command, they are familiar with routine and schedules, and they are used to coming to work in uniforms. In other words, readers would have pulled together all the obvious facts supporting the conclusion—after they knew what the conclusion was.

This explains the reason so many sports enthusiasts are infallible experts on Monday morning, but utter failures when placing their bets on next week's Falcons–Packers game. "It was so obvious *x* would happen. Why didn't the coach see that coming?" The answer is that it was not obvious until it actually happened. Before it happened, there were hundreds of possibilities that might occur and no way to know that any one of them would happened. The answer only seems obvious after we know what the answer is.

Another example: We know that smoking causes cancer. We don't need scientific studies or deep research to recognize this. It is obvious—just plain common sense. Yet this was not common sense in 1950. Sure there were some folks who thought smoking might be bad for our health, but the general consensus was that there really was no issue here. In fact, many thought the opposite was true. I have magazine advertisements from the 1950s touting how Camels will help settle your nerves, and even a doctor announcing that Chesterfields are a swell aid for digestion. Common sense, in 1955, was that cigarettes were a perfectly benign habit. Only after extensive medical research did it become obvious that they were, in fact, killers.

We now look back at the cigarette/cancer connection and wonder how this obvious connection could have been missed before 1964. I'm thinking we'll be saying the same thing in 2025 about permanent brain damage for football players. We'll be shaking our heads in disgust and disbelief, wondering how in the world did the people of 2010 not recognize the obvious results of 300-pound men bashing their heads together for 60 minutes every Sunday? "After all, it's just common sense!" we'll say.

Perhaps there is no better ongoing example of common sense being wrong than in the stock market. The August 14, 2000, edition of *Fortune* magazine listed Ten Stocks to Last the Decade. Of those stocks, two are belly-up, seven finished the decade down, and only one finished higher. Think about the consequences. If the premier financial magazine is unable to pick the biggest winners in the stock market—in fact, most of their picks tanked—what chance does the average Joe have? Once again, we can only be assured of our expertise after the fact. And then it is so obvious who the winners would be.

Even our business schools are not immune from this tendency to predict a horserace after the fact. Years ago, one of the clichéd business case studies featured the air carrier PeopleExpress. The case summary touted the commonsense policies the airline used to make it the fifth largest carrier, and the report raved about the genius of its founder, Donald Burr. Several years later, after the airline's collapse, another case study was making the rounds that described the ignorance of—you guessed it—Donald Burr.

Common sense Here's how to deal with an adversary: Walk a mile in his shoes. If nothing else, you'll be a mile away, and he'll be shoeless.

Summary: The Downside of Common Sense

Think of all the other times you have heard, "We need to do it. After all, it's just common sense." However, recognize some hazards of common sense. Common sense told us that the world is flat, real estate values always increase, and Richard Jewell is a pathetic madman. In each of these cases, common sense was wrong.

In his book *Playback*, Raymond Chandler had this somewhat cynical observation on common sense:

Common sense always speaks too late. Common sense is the guy who tells you you ought to have had your brakes relined last week before you smashed the front end this week. Common sense is the Monday morning quarterback who could have won the ball game if he had been on the team. But he never is. He is high up in the stands with a flask on his hip. Common sense is the little man in a grey suit who never makes a mistake in addition. But it's always somebody else's money he's always adding up.[3]

Common sense is a grand asset to possess, but we need more than one tool in our box, regardless of how sharp that tool may be.

---

[3] Raymond Chandler, *Playback* (Boston: Houghton Miffin, 1958).

Coda

Walking Within a Wise World

Our journey has explored common sense from multiple angles. We've done a pretty thorough job of dissecting the term, but perhaps the best way to identify common sense is—to paraphrase Supreme Court Justice Potter Stewart—by seeing it.

So, let's take a walk through a world of fantasy, fiction, and a couple of drops of reality, where common sense manifests itself in a diverse multitude of pathways.

Lost in the Crowd

A sensible old man, while taking an evening stroll on the white sandy beaches of Pensacola, spotted a young girl involved in a futile endeavor. Standing among hundreds—no, thousands—of starfish that had been trapped when the tide receded, the wide-eyed child was throwing several back into the ocean.

"Silly girl," he called out. "There are thousands of starfish. You can't save them all. What you are doing won't make any difference."

"It will to the ones I save," she replied.

Common sense   Never wrestle with a pig. You both get dirty and the pig kinda likes it.

Takes a Licking and . . .

In the infancy of manned space flight, the National Aeronautics and Space Administration (NASA) encountered a problem that it could not detect in its earth-bound walkthroughs. It seems that neither a ballpoint pen nor a fountain pen would work in the weightlessness of outer space.

The Americans were in a passionate competition with the Soviet Union to demonstrate their country's technological superiority. In a way, our national pride was at stake; NASA was not about to let the Russians pull ahead in any facet of the space race. So NASA scientists, justifiably proud of their engineering talents, sponsored an intense competition to develop a pen that could withstand all the extreme environmental challenges of outer space. After dozens of proposed designs—and $16,000,000 in research—a pen was developed that conquered extreme temperature and pressure changes as well as the absence of gravity.

The Russians, on the other hand, just used a pencil.

Aristotelian Analysis

After a peaceful hike through the pine woodlands, Virgil and his Uncle Sherlock settled in to enjoy a night camping. Sherlock was a philosophy professor at the local community college and Virgil looked forward to gaining his perspective on life while soaking up the splendor of the Blue Ridge Mountains.

They set up their tent, enjoyed a fine gourmet stew and a vintage bottle of RC Cola, then went right to sleep. Virgil awoke several hours later and nudged his learned uncle. "Sherlock, look up and tell me what you see."

A groggy Sherlock responded, "I see millions and millions of stars."

"And what does that tell you?" Virgil asked.

The professor pondered the many profound possibilities and then replied, "Well, astronomically, it tells me there are millions of galaxies and potentially billions of planets. Astrologically, I observe Saturn is in Leo. Meteorologically, I predict we will have a beautiful day tomorrow. Horologically, I deduce the time is approximately a quarter past three. Theologically, I see that God is all-powerful and we are but a small and insignificant part of the universe." Sherlock sighed and then turned to his nephew. "What does it tell you, Virgil?"

Virgil was silent for a moment, letting his uncle's wise words soak in. "Well, Uncle Sherlock, all that is probably true. But seeing all those stars tells me just one thing. Somebody's done stole our tent."

▨ **Common sense** Use the as-if principle: "If you want a quality, act as if you already have it." —*William James*

Outside the Box

While wandering the hallways of the corporate offices, I walked into the middle of a seminar designed to teach young executives how to think. The instructor was presenting an exercise I had witnessed umpteen times. You know the one. You are given a sheet of paper containing nine dots arranged in three rows of three. You are then instructed to connect the dots by drawing no more than four straight lines without lifting your pencil from the paper. Although first finding the puzzle impossible, you learn that the solution is to extend your lines past the square boundaries suggested by the dots, thus allowing you to approach from a different angle. The instructor will then puff out his chest and proudly announce that the exercise has taught you how to "think outside the box."

Because he was an old friend, I decided to have a little fun with the trainer and offer a few alternate solutions. One was to roll the paper into a cone and connect the dots in a single spiraling line. Another involves folding the paper so all the dots were stacked up and then stab a pencil through the pile-o-dots. I also put the paper on the copy machine and reduced the image until it was all one big smudge—and then used a wide marker to draw a single line across the splotch.

I pulled my friend aside and showed him my alternate solutions. His forehead furrowed as he scolded me: "Oh no, Ken, that's not how it's done. You sit down there quietly and I'll show you the proper way solve the puzzle."

As I walked away, I was baffled by the idea that the most-often used exercise for teaching people how to think outside the box required the participants to adhere to a specific solution.

A Drop in the Bucket

Michele was excited with the purchase she made while walking through the Chattanooga River Walk Flea Market—an Arizona prickly pear cactus. Although it did look great in her sunroom, like many flea market finds, it did not come with instructions and Michele had no idea how to care for the exotic plant. She was especially concerned with how much water to give it; she knew it would drown if she matched what she gave to her native plants.

So Michele did what all other children of modern technology do: she googled, and a massive amount of information rained down on her. She had her choice of calculations, detailed analysis of climatology, and myriad watering schedules, but everything seemed so complicated. All she wanted to do was water a plant!

Michele was getting frustrated with all the overkill when she suddenly thought of the antidote for her problem. She put her watering plan into effect and has seen the cactus thrive ever since.

The antidote? Each day, Michele checks the weather report for Phoenix. Whenever it rains there, she gives her plant the same amount of water.

▓ **Common sense** "Rank is responsibility not privilege." —*Peter Drucker*

The Millionaire

The captain walked around Station 27, personally serving each of her firefighters second helpings of that night's dinner treat—cheese jambalaya. As the dinner progressed, the conversation morphed into the firefighters' fantasy regarding what they would do if they won that weekend's mega-lottery and became very rich. Talks of yachts, sports cars, mansions—even owning a Major League Baseball franchise—filled the firehouse that evening. It seemed each person's fantasy outdid the last, until it was Jeff's turn. "You know," he said quietly, "I really don't think my life would change much." But before he could be completely drowned out by the jeers he added, "Except maybe I'd buy me a half gallon of butter pecan ice cream and eat it all by myself."

No firefighter had their number drawn that weekend. But, three days later, as the same group sat down to a mountain of barbecue ribs, the captain pulled Jeff aside and presented him with a half gallon of butter pecan ice cream and a spoon. His fellow firefighters had collected six bucks and made Jeff—at least by his definition—a very rich man.

Dear Abby

While meandering through an old newspaper, I ran across what is perhaps the most famous advice ever given by the columnist Dear Abby (or was it Ann Landers?). She was asked:

"I'd love to get my degree, but it would take five years and I would be fifty-one years old when I get out of college. Should I go back to school?"

Abby/Ann replied: "How old will you be in five years if you don't go back to college?"

The Long Walk Home

A long-haul trucker in a 14-wheeler drove under a bridge that was just a couple of inches lower than the top of his rig. His truck was wedged so tightly under that bridge that he couldn't back it out. Traffic was jammed for miles.

Police and firefighters arrived on the scene, as did county officials and engineers, who proposed dozens of options for dislodging the truck. The one that met with the most favor was to destroy the bridge to get the rig free and unsnarl the traffic. Then one small boy in the crowd asked his mom, "Why don't they just let the air out of the tires?"

How to Succeed in Business

Sam Battistone walked into the presidency of one of the nation's largest restaurant chains by the time he was thirty-one years old. How did he do it? Sam explains:

> When I was eight years old, I mopped floors and cleaned tables in one of my father's restaurants, and when I was ten I washed maybe a thousand dishes a night. When I was sixteen, I managed one of my father's restaurants and by the time I was eighteen I was working a hundred hours a week overseeing a dozen of them. I served long hours in real estate, marketing, and even the finance department, giving up all the activities a normal twenty-year-old would enjoy just so I could make my father's company the strongest in the industry. So, you want to know how to become the president of a major corporation by the time you are thirty-one years old? *Get yourself a father who owns a chain of restaurants.*

Common sense   Eagles may soar, but weasels don't get sucked into jet engines.

Grasping the Real Goal

Kent was hiking through the Smoky Mountains with his friend Nick. As they were soaking in the nature experience, the pathway turned sharply and they came face to face with the cutest little bear cub you could ever imagine. While Kent was taken aback, Nick showed no hesitation. "Hey little feller," he cooed as he bounced the baby bear on his knee. "Whatcha doin' out here all by yourself?"

Just as Kent advised, "I don't think that is a real good idea, Nick," a roar came from about a hundred yards away. It was Momma Bear and she was not happy.

Nick gently set the cub down and then took off running. Kent yelled some good advice to him, "Nick! You can't outrun that bear!" to which Nick replied over his shoulder, "I don't have to outrun that bear. I just have to outrun you."

Perspective

True story. On the eve of my 50th birthday, I took a stroll through Piedmont Park, contemplating the final decades of my life. As the trail turned around a large boulder, a frog jumped in my path and sat directly in front of me. And then something odd happened; the frog spoke.

"Please sir, hear my plea." I must confess, the frog did have my attention.

"I am not really a frog, but a beautiful princess. A wicked witch cast a spell on me and turned me into this greasy green monster. But, if you will kiss me, I will turn back into a beautiful princess and"—here comes the really good part—"serve you completely for the rest of your life." And then I'd swear the frog winked at me.

"Well I'll be darned," I said as I reached down and picked up the frog. I smiled at my good fortune, put the frog in my pocket, then resumed my walk.

"What are you doing?" exclaimed the princess/frog from my pocket. "Didn't you hear me? Kiss me, princess, serve you. Didn't you hear what I said?"

"Yeah, I heard you," I replied. "It's just at this time in my life, I think I'd rather have a talking frog."

░ **Common sense** *Whether designing systems, raising a child, or preparing a recipe, make it easy to do the right thing; make it hard to do the wrong thing.*

Panthers Above, Vipers Below

A joyful young girl was taking a peaceful morning walk through a grassland when she noticed a panther creeping behind her. She then glanced over her other shoulder and noticed yet another panther. Both were obviously stalking her for lunch.

Terrified, she bolted over a hill, only to find a cliff awaiting her. There seemed to be no escape from the pursuing predators, but the right then she noticed a thick vine hanging over the cliff. At the last second, she escaped their snarling jaws by climbing down the vine.

As she slid down the vine, her heart stopped in fear. There, below, where the vine met the ground, were dozens of water moccasins, looking up at her angrily.

So what did she do? She looked beside her and noticed there was yet another vine, this one supporting a single, luscious strawberry. She picked the succulent fruit and chewed on the momentary sweetness life had delivered.

***** ***** *****

Common sense takes many forms and shapes and colors and genres. You will see it all around you as you walk along life's journey. Soak it in.

Index

I

Y, Z

Other Apress Business Titles You Will Find Useful

Firing at Will
Shepherd
978-1-4302-3738-9

No-Drama Project Management
Gerardi
978-1-4302-3990-1

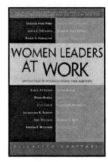

Women Leaders at Work
Ghaffari
978-1-4302-3729-7

Managing Humans, 2nd Edition
Lopp
978-1-4302-4314-4

Tech Job Hunt Handbook
Grossman
978-1-4302-4548-3

Fixing and Flipping Real Estate
Boardman
978-1-4302-4644-2

When to Hire—or Not Hire—a Consultant
Orr/Orr
978-1-4302-4734-0

Reasonably Simple Economics
Osborne
978-1-4302-5941-1

Underwater
Lauer
978-1-4302-4470-7

Available at www.apress.com